Early Childhood
An Introductory Text

GW00505945

Early Childhood
An Introductory Text

Nóirín Hayes

Gill & Macmillan

Published in Ireland by
Gill & Macmillan Ltd
Goldenbridge
Dublin 8
with associated companies throughout the world

© Nóirín Hayes 1993
0 7171 2053 8
Design and illustrations by Duo Design, Dublin
Photographs by Moya Nolan
Print origination by
Seton Music Graphics Ltd, Bantry, Co. Cork
Printed by ColourBooks, Dublin

A catalogue record for this book is
available from the British Library.

To
Mike, Clare, Kate and Ali

CONTENTS

introduction

'The best way to prepare a person for life is to give him a zest for life.'
(*E. Lawrence*)

For many years I have taught students who, on graduating, go on to work with young children in a variety of different settings. The subject areas I teach include those I believe to be most important to anyone hoping to work with young children — child development and early childhood education. Over the years I have found it difficult to identify a textbook which addresses these topics in an engaging and clear manner while at the same time presenting an Irish dimension. I hope this introductory text will redress the balance. It is intended for students who are training to work with young children or who, in their work, will have contact with young children and their families. The primary aim of the book is to inform, stimulate and alert students to the important aspects of their work and to the value of this work — a value that we must recognise ourselves before we can expect others to recognise it. I hope it will spur the reader on to more extensive reading and study.

My background, my life experiences and my training have shaped this book. There are certain basic views I hold which underpin the content and the emphasis of the book.

- First and most important I hold the child as *central*. Each child is an individual and we must have the time and the interest and the knowledge to be able to allow for this individuality in all our work.

- Secondly I believe that the child is *good*. No child is born bad, although many are born with considerable disadvantages. It is essential that early childhood workers believe this. Underpinning a lot of our more rigid practices and punitive styles is the belief that children need to be taught to be good. Rather they need to be rewarded for behaving as we expect them to and assisted in understanding why certain behaviours are considered inappropriate.

- Thirdly I consider that the *interaction* between different aspects of development at different stages must not be lost sight of by our tendency to segment the child as we try to unravel the influences that shape her* life.

- Fourthly I believe that the child is an *active agent* in her learning rather than a passive receiver of information. This belief has serious implications for practice and requires that adults allow children the freedom to make mistakes, solve problems and find solutions rather than interfering and showing children how to 'draw the cat' or 'cut out the picture'.

- Fifthly I believe in the *importance* of the early years. I do not hold the extreme view that there is no hope for change after the child has reached, say, seven. However, I do believe that the foundation for much future learning, behaviour and success is laid down in the very early experiences of a child. It is unacceptable to say that a trauma will affect a young child less than an older one simply because they do not appear to understand it — it is this very fact of childhood understanding that makes early experiences so important and that

* I have chosen to use the title 'she' when referring to the individual child.

places an important obligation on early childhood workers to be sensitive to children's experiences and how they might be affecting them. This sensitivity requires that you recognise that what something means to you may not mean the same to a child.

- Finally, I believe in the powerful *role of the adult* in the young child's life. Adults are significant in that they can expand the experiences and the horizons of the child during the early years by their attention, interests, listening skills, observations and the provision of opportunity. Adults must, of course, recognise their limitations also. There are environmental influences and the influence of other adults, for example, that will prevail in certain circumstances.

This book is intended for those who will work with young children as their career, it is intended for those who wish to work as au pairs or nannies, childminders and in playgroups, naíonraí, preschools, nurseries and, indeed, in the junior cycle of the primary school. It aims to raise a wide variety of issues, some more pertinent to one type of childcare facility than another.

The overriding belief behind the book is that to work well with, and for children you must understand them; to understand them there are certain basic facts to be learned but most of all you must continue to be surprised by and curious about children. You must always be open to learning from them. One of the great joys of working with young children is that their whole being can be seen through their behaviour, the way they think, the way they interact, the way they look at the world — quite differently, it appears, from the way adults do.

Our own past experience as children is one aspect of our environment that seems to have a deep effect on our behaviour with children. Unwittingly we may hear ourselves use an expression that our parents used with us and we may not even believe what we are saying but it seems to come from deep within. We all hold strong views and expectations about how children should behave and what they should and shouldn't do — often reflecting our own experiences. We must make efforts to bring these expectations to the level of consciousness and work through them so that we understand, as far as possible, what directs the way we behave. Personal experiences, those both empowering and stagnating, must be addressed in a personal way by each individual. This is not something that is easily done but it must remain as a task of significant importance. As you work through the material in this book it will be worth thinking of it in the context of your own experiences and expectations.

The book aims to:

- broaden the knowledge base of the reader

- introduce issues of importance to working with young children

- identify skills necessary for working with young children

- present practical training in an accessible way.

Perhaps the main aim of this book is to encourage a common approach to practice — an approach that is interactive, developmentally appropriate and truly child-centred and one that lends itself to collaboration and discussion with peers, parents and other professionals. The transfer of the theory into practice, however, may vary considerably according to the type of service and the training of the adults. This book aims to lead to an approach to practice that does not get caught up by the constraints of space, order, routine, that is provided by adults who facilitate development in individual children, who recognise the dynamics and influence of the group, who provide wide-ranging, multi-media, appropriate experiences and who continue to question and review practice and progress regularly.

Warmth, spontaneity and flexibility exist better in a well-planned environment focusing on children than in a come-day-go-day environment. Both may offer the child safety and short-term benefits but only the former can truly enable, stimulate and challenge the young child because it is only in the former that we, the adults, can evaluate practice and learn from our children. A degree of structure is not only desirable but essential for the provision of good quality care.

A brief word about what is not included in the book. As well as an understanding of child development, and an interest in children, anyone working with young children must have a well-grounded background in child health, hygiene and safety. All the theory in the world is as nothing if the health and safety of children and adults is compromised. For historical reasons the subject of early childhood care and education has tended to be equated with health rather than education. As a result there are many books and articles on the subject of health and safety. No book can be all things to everyone and this is no exception: the issue of health and safety is not covered but the expectation is that the reader will acquire the relevant information and skills through the wide variety of sources available. The book discusses practice in terms of child development and provides a series of exercises and activities. There are many good books that present ideas and ways of doing different activities with young children and some of these are included in the list of suggested further reading at the end of the book.

The book contains eleven chapters and is laid out in the following way:

Chapter 1 reviews the historical influences that led to the rise of interest and study in early childhood care and education in general, and in Ireland in particular.

Chapter 2 considers the role of adults in the lives of children. It also reviews the different approaches and methods used in the study of children.

Chapter 3 discusses the important role of observation in allowing us to see beyond the immediate behaviour of the child. It explores the process by which we can use our knowledge of child development to explain and understand the behaviour of young children.

Chapters 4–8 are concerned with child development and cover the different aspects of this development. While these chapters describe the progress of development under separate headings it is important to remember that different aspects of development interact with each other and the individual child must be considered as a whole. This emphasis on interaction and influence reflects an holistic approach to child development and takes account of the complexity of that development.

Chapter 9 reviews the possible causes of unwanted behaviour in young children and discusses different approaches to encouraging good behaviour.

Chapter 10 addresses the subject of play in the early years. This period in a child's life is one where play has an important role and is one of the key paths to learning for the child. This chapter describes play and discusses it in the overall context of the learning of young children and the role of adults.

Chapter 11 links theory to practice. It suggests ways to apply our developmental knowledge to the provision of good quality early childhood care and education. Each chapter contains a summary and exercises. The book concludes with a list of further reading, references and a glossary of terms.

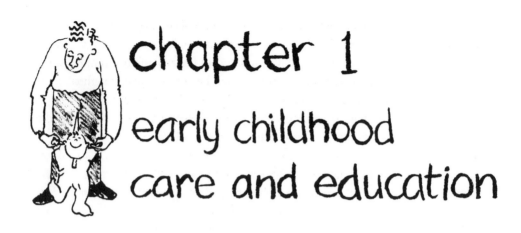

chapter 1
early childhood
care and education

HISTORICAL PERSPECTIVES IN EARLY CHILDHOOD

In any study of children and their development it is useful to look back over history and see how the circumstances of the time influenced particular theories or views about children. This influence of the time is called the *zeitgeist*, or the 'spirit of the time' and is an important concept to bear in mind when reviewing the opinions and views of others. For instance in relation to young children, over the last century there have been debates about the relative merit of breastfeeding over bottlefeeding. These debates have often been informed as much by fashion as common sense and for those interested in children and the effect different factors in the environment have on their development it is essential to bear in mind what societal factors may be at work at the time any particular theory or explanation of behaviour is proposed. This is as much true of the present as the past but it seems to be much more difficult to analyse these effects when one is living through the process. Despite the difficulty it is worth trying to achieve an understanding of the various factors that influence the way people were thinking about children in the past and are thinking about children now.

CHILDHOOD — A DISTINCT PERIOD OF DEVELOPMENT?

The notion that childhood should be considered as a unique and distinct period of development requiring different treatment and attention from adults is of relatively recent origin. A study carried out by Phillipe Aries offers an interesting history of childhood. He points out that in mediaeval times there was little value placed on childhood. Indeed it was not considered a separate phase of development and children were considered to be little adults. The infant might or might not survive and was of little value to the community. Up to the mid-nineteenth century the death rate among children was high. Women had many pregnancies but only a percentage of their children survived. This affected the importance placed on the young child — it was emotionally draining to invest too much in a child until you could be sure that the child would live. As issues of health and medicine improved there was an increased likelihood that both mother and child would survive pregnancy. As a result more attention was given to the baby from the very beginning and a move towards the regulation of the number of children began. We are still being influenced by the effects of improved medical technology on family life at this point in our development as a society. In medieval times, by the time the child could walk and talk she was seen as an active member of society equivalent to older children and adults and often treated as an adult. Adults assumed that children were smaller versions of themselves and the concept of age, for example, had little meaning for most children and adults unaware of their exact age or date of birth! There were no special toys or games manufactured for children as there are now. Indeed those games and toys that did exist were for the enjoyment of all and many pictures and portraits from medieval times show adults enjoying a game of marbles or 'jacks'.

EARLY CHILDREARING PRACTICES

In previous centuries poorer children were seen as tools for the adults — chimney boys and mill workers. In wealthier families children were very much seen and not heard. Portraits show them as small adults dressed in miniature adult-type clothes. Many were brought up by nannies and tutors and had little close contact with parents, often having all their meals in the 'nursery'!

The seventeenth century marked the beginning of a change in attitudes towards children. The religious beliefs of the time were influential in this change of view. The concept of original sin gave rise to the idea of the child as a creature needing to be trained, reformed and saved. Children were considered to be born stubborn, unsocial and evil and it was the responsibility of the adult to direct them from the influence of the devil. This was done by training them in the customs and expectations of the day. Harsh authoritarian childrearing practices were recommended to transform these bad, corrupted children into good, God-fearing citizens. Schools emphasised moral training and disobedience often resulted in beatings. This puritanical approach, as it is often called, is well recorded in both factual accounts and fiction of the time. It is unlikely that all children were treated in this way but it was the prevailing view of childhood. It is, I believe, worth mentioning that the debates and recommendations regarding the training and education of children at this period were specifically meant to refer to the male children of the middle and upper classes. No such concern was shown for the poorer boys or for any girls.

SOME IMPORTANT NAMES

The focus for the adult was the need to educate the child in the moral code and to ensure that children were literate. Indeed it was the necessity for a literate workforce, following the Industrial Revolution, that is often credited with the growth of education in general. The seventeenth century saw also the emergence of the Enlightenment, the age of reason, where greater emphasis was placed on logical thinking with less reliance on superstition and magic. This led to a move towards a philosophy of reason emphasising the importance of human dignity and the value of respect for the human. Revised concepts of childhood gradually led to a significant change in the way children were treated.

John Locke (1632–1704) was an influential British philosopher. He proposed that children's minds were like blank slates, or *tabula rasa*. Children were not born evil, he argued, they were not formed, mentally, at all. Locke saw the parent/adult as a key agent in the education of the child and argued that by careful use of reward and punishment, imitation and repetition, children would be receptive to and influenced by this experience. Mankind was seen as rational and children were considered as lacking the necessary experience and knowledge for appropriate social behaviour. Locke was a humane man, opposed to physical punishment because it did not foster self-control but rather engendered fear. His views were influential in the gradual move away from punitive treatment of children and towards the more compassionate approach we see today. As well as influencing trends in childrearing and education Locke also had an influence on the very young discipline of psychology, the study of behaviour. He is regarded as one of the earliest *Behaviourists*, that school of psychology which emphasises the importance and the power of the environment. Behaviourists consider that adults have a powerful role in directing and influencing the development and education of young children. This model of psychology will be discussed in some detail at a later stage.

Jean Jacques Rousseau (1712–1778) was a French philosopher who proposed a theory of childhood emphasising the natural goodness of children. He disagreed with Locke's view that children were blank slates at birth and considered children as basically good by nature with an intuitive knowledge of what was right and wrong. He also considered them naturally inclined towards positive healthy growth. In his important book on education *Émile,* he wrote '. . . the child that man raises is almost certain to be inferior to the child that nature raises'.

In relation to education Rousseau argued that:

- The social environment might impede the natural development of the child and he proposed that children be educated by specially trained tutors.

- Individual tuition rather than school-based education was most effective and he did not allow, in his theory, for the social nature of the child.

- The child actively participates in his development by actively engaging the environment and using it to suit his interests. The child was considered an active, busy, testing and motivated explorer and not a passive recipient of information.

- Children require different experiences and treatment at different stages in their childhood and he identified four such stages — infancy, childhood, late childhood and adolescence. This approach is so commonplace now that it is hard to imagine it was not always the view.

Rousseau emphasised that children go through a process of maturation from one stage to the next. Each child was seen as unique and account of this was to be taken in the education of children from the earliest moment. As the first author to propose this developmental view of childhood he can be regarded as one of the earliest child psychologists in the *developmental* tradition — followed by such influential thinkers as Piaget who will be discussed at greater length in the chapter on children's thinking.

Charles Darwin (1809–1882) was one of the most influential students of nature. By the mid-nineteenth century the age of reason was well established and a lot of time and money was spent finding out more about the world in which we live. Darwin, from his studies, proposed the theory of evolution in his book *The Origin of the Species* in 1859. Fundamental to this theory is the idea of the survival of the fittest — an idea that has influenced many of the theories of childhood to emerge at the turn of the century.

At another level Darwin should be considered important in the history of early childhood care and education. He published the diary of his observations of his son — a baby biography — in 1877. Here he had recorded in detail his observations of the development of his son from his earliest days. It was not a scientific analysis of development but rather a descriptive piece. Nonetheless it paved the way for many more baby biographies and led to a growth in the use of observation as a method of child study. It also gave rise to the design of studies that take account of development over a period of time. These are called longitudinal studies.

SOCIAL AND EDUCATIONAL CHANGE

As well as the influence of individual thinkers and changing trends in philosophy and psychology there were other factors that affected the way we now regard childhood. These can be considered under the headings of social and educational change and are inextricably linked to the changes of thought outlined above.

The **Industrial Revolution** is seen as just that — a revolution. It is regarded as a definite point of social change. It led to the growth of cities and large towns and, consequently to greater urbanisation, suburbanisation and localised poverty, both urban and rural. This led to, among other things, a growing problem of unsupervised young children or street urchins. This is well described by the authors of the day including Charles Dickens.

In other cases the only option open to families in poverty was to send children, and mothers, out working. The type of work children did varied and depended on the industry in the area. Children's work included farm labouring, mill working, mine working and chimney sweeping.

Both these factors — the growing numbers of street urchins and the rise in the number of young children working — led to changes in social legislation and mark the beginnings of state support for early childhood services.

There were two particularly influential pieces of social legislation in the nineteenth century. The first was the Factories Act in its various forms passed during the nineteenth century which placed restrictions on employers with regard to the age of children employed, the hours they could work and the type of work they could do. In the main, child labour is now a thing of the past in our society but there are still many societies today where child labour is a fact of life.

The second piece of legislation to have an impact on the treatment of young children was the Education Act of 1870. This Act gave parents a right of admission for their under five-year-old children to education, with the compulsory school age — that is the age at which children must attend school — set at five years of age. (With the establishment of the Irish State and the Irish Constitution the compulsory school age was changed to, and remains, six years .)

These acts were English but at the time of their enactment influenced the situation in Ireland as we were still under English jurisdiction. In fact the education issue in Ireland was a very political one. One of the consequences of this was that a network of national schools accepting children, sometimes as young as three, was initiated in 1831 and well established by the 1840s.

EUROPEAN TRENDS

While these changes in social legislation were occurring there were, throughout Europe, a number of important early educators emerging. These included **Pestalozzi** (1745–1827), a Swiss educator of significant influence. Pestalozzi developed a system of education in which he emphasised the importance of teaching children in terms of their interests. He did not stress formal education of children until they were six or seven as he regarded them as too young to be able to grasp more abstract information. Pestalozzi himself was not as successful as some of his followers in putting his educational theory into practice but his ideas about early education still have influence. Pestalozzi was significant because of his direct influence on certain people.

Unlike Rousseau, who wrote about his philosophy of childhood and education, Pestalozzi tried to put his ideas into practice. He established Pestalozzian schools at Burghof and Yverdon where the care and education of young children were very much a part of the life of the community and they were part of the community also. They harvested crops, made bread, wove yarn and made cloth. The intention was, that through ordinary and useful experiences, children would learn skills and acquire knowledge in a more meaningful way.

THE PESTALOZZI LEGACY

Pestalozzi's educational experiment attracted a wide variety of visitors including Robert Owen, from Scotland, Friedrich Froebel from Germany and, perhaps surprisingly, a John Synge from Ireland. These and others took the Pestalozzian ideas and applied them — with their own modifications — to their own practice.

Robert Owen, influenced by what he saw when he visited Pestalozzi, decided to put the ideas into practice. He provided nursery education for the young children of the adults working at his mill in New Lanark, Scotland, as early as 1816. He was quite clear in his view that young children were to be treated with respect, not beaten and not forced into formal education at too early an age. The classroom environment was to be bright and hung with pictures. Materials were to be of interest to children and the experience of attending class was to be fun. There was singing, music and dance but no teaching of reading, writing or arithmetic in a formal way until the children were six or seven years old.

Unfortunately for early childhood education, Owen was a socialist and an atheist and despite the fact that he was a rich and influential figure, he fell into disfavour. As a result, his ideas about early education did not have the wide-ranging effect they might have had. In fact, early education in the infant classes of mid-nineteenth-century England, and Ireland, was quite different to that proposed by Owen. Records describe classes of up to 100 children of differing ages in tiered classes learning through drill and rote. The task of the single teacher was very difficult under these circumstances and it is certain that the experience cannot have been enjoyable or enriching for either pupils or teachers.

Friedrich Froebel (1782–1852), an important influence on early childhood practice, also visited Pestalozzi. Unlike Owen, who visited for a short time, Froebel worked in the Pestalozzian school on a number of occasions. Indeed it was through these experiences that he committed the rest of his life to the education of children. Taking with him many ideas from Pestalozzi, and in the light of his own belief in the importance of nature and man's place in nature, Froebel developed a detailed philosophy of education and applied this in the various schools he ran. In the beginning he concentrated on the education of older children but over time he began to realise the importance of early experiences to later learning.

Froebel was one of the first authors to recognise the important role of parents, particularly the mother, in the education of the child. Indeed he wrote pamphlets to encourage mothers to play more with their children and he developed a series of songs for mothers to sing. He believed that continuity between home and school was important and stressed that adults learn from children as children learn from adults. 'Let us live with our children, let them live with us, so shall we gain through them what all of us need.'

Furthermore, Froebel believed that women as well as men should be involved in the education of children. This was a revolutionary stance at the time and Froebel was forced to establish a training school for women as none existed. Here he trained the first *kindergarten* teachers. The word kindergarten means 'children's garden'. It has another meaning also: on the one hand it captures the notion of children as part of nature, to be nurtured and enriched by the surrounding environment; on the other it emphasises the importance of nature and things natural to the educational experiences of children. Froebel considered that children were the most important agents in their own learning. He was the first educationalist to emphasise the importance of a 'child-centred' approach in education. He believed that children should be actively involved in learning and he encouraged teachers not to teach children but to be led by the interests of children when providing learning opportunities. He emphasised the role of play in the process of learning — '. . . at this age play is never trivial; it is serious and deeply significant. The focus of play at this age is the core of the whole future'. In line with his view of the natural unfolding of development and the differences in children at different stages, he developed a series of toys and games — gifts — to facilitate learning. These gifts — balls, boards, sand, clay and so on were intended to tap into the different interests and abilities of children at different stages. Interestingly, when it was felt that teachers were relying too heavily on these gifts and treating them as tasks to be completed by a particular age rather than as a source of interest and learning for the child, they were rejected and are no longer used.

Froebel's views on children, their natural position in the order of things, his recognition of the value and importance of childhood in itself, his views on the role of adults as guides, facilitators and learners have influenced both early education and primary education over the last century. In Ireland in particular the broad philosophy of child-centred education that underlies the current primary curriculum owes much to Froebel's own work and the work of those he influenced.

Maria Montessori (1870–1952) was another influential, international thinker in the field of early childhood care and education. In the beginning Montessori trained as a doctor and indeed was the first woman doctor to graduate from her college in Rome. Her early work was with the poor and socially deprived children of Rome. Many of the children she worked with would also have had a mental handicap. As a doctor her practice with young children owes something to the influence of other doctors, particularly one — Eduard Seguin. In his work with mentally handicapped and mentally

ill patients he developed certain tasks which encouraged their development. These tasks were graded according to the ability of the individual patient. This idea of graded tasks, carefully designed to develop certain skills, at different stages of development, was an important influence on Montessori when she came to design materials for her school. Unlike Froebel, who emphasised the school and home as linked in community towards the education of children, Montessori stressed the need for a specially prepared environment in which children would learn. She regarded childhood as a state to be protected and allowed to develop in a separate, 'planned' environment that 'protects the child from the difficult and dangerous obstacles that threaten him/her in the adult world. The shelter in the storm, the oasis in the desert, the place of spiritual rest ought to be created in the world precisely to assure the healthy development of the child'. Montessori, unlike Froebel, saw childhood as a separate state, apart from adulthood and existing in its own right.

In line with Pestalozzi and Froebel, Montessori saw development as the unfolding of a biologically predetermined programme. She identified stages of particular sensitivity where, she argued, different skills and concepts were acquired more readily than at other stages. In her planned environment she provided materials that were carefully designed to help the child develop along the programmed path and her method provides a clear sequence of activities to be followed exactly. Montessori wrote that play was the centre of a child's work but she defined play narrowly in terms of that which was preparatory to adult life needs. She saw little value in imaginative or fantasy play and as a result nursery rhymes, fairytales and so on did not feature in her method. This strictness of approach would be opposed by most workers in the field of early education today, who would regard the fantasy world of childhood, as an important element in their overall development.

Despite criticisms of her method, Montessori has made a significant contribution to the field of early childhood care and education, particularly, in relation to the idea of scaled furniture and much of the sensorial equipment found in nurseries and preschools today. Also important was the wealth of her writing about childhood, which has led to a respect for this period of development, which was sadly lacking when she began her pioneering work at the turn of the century. Montessori's work with young children in Rome was very successful and the success of her method led to a growth of interest which is still widespread today. This is particularly the case in Ireland, where to many people, the word Montessori is almost synonomous with early education.

— AND IN IRELAND?

In Ireland the influence of the Enlightenment and the impact of the Industrial Revolution were tempered by the political reality of the time. Education was seen as a means of suppressing nationalistic notions and little serious thought was given to the age of children attending school or the appropriateness of the curriculum. There were, however, some isolated innovations. **John Synge**, a relative of the author John Millington Synge, visiting Pestalozzi from Ireland in 1815, was greatly influenced by the ideas underlying the education provided in his school. On his return to Ireland he, like Robert Owen, established a school on his estate at Glanmore Castle, Roundwood, County Wicklow. It appears that the school was run on child-centred lines with a focus on teaching through the use of materials and experiences that were of interest to the children. The day was divided between classroom instruction and work on the land. The school did not last long and the influence on other schools and practice in general seems to have been slight.

Another Irish educationalist who took on the idea of active involvement of children in their own learning was **Maria Edgeworth** (1767–1849). She wrote many books on different topics, among them one, co-authored with her father, entitled *Essays on Practical Education,* in which she stressed the importance of the home to the education of the child. Maria had been responsible for the upbringing and education of her younger sisters and as a result had written a series of children's stories. She had these published for the benefit of parents whom she considered the primary educators of children.

Froebel education in Ireland: In 1862 the first recorded Froebel kindergarten was opened in Dublin by a Miss Herbert. She had trained with Froebel and her kindergarten put into practice the philosophy of child-centred and play-based learning. Miss Herbert may have trained a number of staff at her kindergarten. In a Department of Education publication of 1888 there is reference to a training course leading to a Kindergarten Certificate being provided at Marlborough Street, Dublin. The focus of this course was, however, on the exercises proposed by Froebel to improve hand/eye co-ordination and manual dexterity rather than on his general philosophy of education.

In 1918 Froebel training began at Alexandra College in Dublin. There was a variety of courses on offer from a one year certificate course for junior schoolteachers and governesses to the three year Froebel teacher training course that is standard now. In 1921 there were nine students studying Froebel education at the college. It was decided to close the Alexandra College Froebel training course in 1970.

In 1934 a Froebel kindergarten training course was run by the Dominican Sisters in Belfast. From this grew an interest in Froebel training in Ireland and in 1943 the Dominican Sisters at Sion Hill in Blackrock, Dublin, decided to organise a training course. This was followed by more courses and a great growth in interest and attendance. In 1960 the Department of Education came to an agreement with the Froebel training college and, as a result, its graduates from the three year training course became recognised and eligible to apply for positions as teachers in all primary schools.

In addition to the undergraduate Froebel courses on offer at Sion Hill the college also ran a one year graduate training course. The Froebel training college is still providing training and most graduates find employment within the primary school system although a number may choose to open private kindergartens.

Montessori education in Ireland: In 1919 two Irish women — a Mercy nun, Sr Gertrude Allman, and Mrs Eleonora Gibbons — attended the first Montessori training course held in London. Both women came from Waterford. On her return Sr Gertrude started the first Montessori class in Ireland in 1920.

In 1927 Montessori visited Ireland for the first time when she came to Waterford. She visited Ireland a number of times during the 1930s including a visit to a training course at the Sacred Heart Convent, Leeson Street, Dublin in 1938. On this visit she was accompanied by two English colleagues who were to have an influence on the development of Montessori training in Ireland, Miss Homfrey and Miss Child. In 1946 an Irish branch of the Association Montessori International (AMI) was established and in 1949 a one year evening course was offered by the Dominican Sisters at Sion Hill. By 1957 they were running a two year full-time course. The training offered at Sion Hill was extended in 1965 to include a one year graduate course and the full-time course now takes three years to complete. The AMI Montessori training college is now located in Milltown, Dublin.

In 1970 Miss Homfrey and Miss Child were invited to a meeting of the recently formed Irish Pre-school Playgroups Association. They had founded the St Nicholas Montessori Training Centre in London and spoke about their experiences. The meeting was attended by, among others, Sighle Fitzgerald. Shortly after the meeting she invited interested people to discuss the possibility of setting up a St Nicholas Montessori Society in Ireland. Her efforts were successful and in 1971–72 a part-time evening diploma course was offered. In 1979 the St Nicholas Montessori Society bought their present premises in Dun Laoghaire and in 1984 the first full-time day course started.

Since 1984 there has been a growth in Montessori training courses. In that year the London Montessori began offering courses and they are located in Holles Street, Dublin. In 1987 two former members of the St Nicholas Montessori Society of Ireland founded the Montessori Education Centre at Nth Great George's Street, Dublin and they offer a wide range of courses.

Most people trained in the Montessori method work in the area of early education or special education. Unlike Froebel training it is not recognised by the Department of Education and so students are not eligible to work within the national school system although some will find positions in private primary schools.

In response to a proposal from OMEP—the World Organisation for Early Childhood Education—the Dublin Institute of Technology at Cathal Brugha Street established a wide-ranging training course in the area of early childhood care and education. This course was started in 1979. Initially a one-year course, it is now a two-year certificate course. The college also offers a Diploma in Early Childhood Care and Education, open to graduates from the certificate course and to others with appropriate or equivalent qualifications and experience.

Steiner education in Ireland: The philosopher and educationalist **Rudolph Steiner**, with the support of the Waldorf Foundation, established the first Steiner school in Germany in 1919. The philosophy behind the system recognises in each child a unique spiritual individuality emerging as the child progresses through to adulthood. Each stage is seen to require a different approach. Steiner considered that education should lead the child towards clarity of thought, strength of will and sensitivity of feeling.

Though Steiner himself recommended that children remain at home for their first seven years most schools now provide a kindergarten for children from four years. The kindergarten is seen as an extension of the home in which children can develop in line with their natural tendencies. There is an emphasis on play with non-structured materials; toys provided are made from organic and natural materials and are simple and unformed. This is to leave as much scope as possible for the child to activate her own imagination. No pre-reading or pre-writing exercises are introduced at the kindergarten stage.

There has been a Steiner school in Belfast since the mid 1970s and one in County Clare since 1984. In 1986 a group of parents in Dublin formed a group and opened their first school in 1988. They are based in Maxwell Road, Rathmines.

Barnardos in Ireland: Thomas Barnardo was born in Dame Street in Dublin in 1845. In 1866 he moved to London to study medicine. It was during this period that he became aware of the poverty among children and was horrified by the fact that there were homeless children sleeping on the streets. Initially Barnardo focused his attention on the needs of boys. He opened his first residential home in London in 1874. Not only did he feed and clothe the boys but he also organised training for them so that they might find employment. By this time Barnardo had begun to recognise that there were many young girls in need of support and he began to provide services for them also.

In the mid 1960s Barnardos established its first base in Ireland. Barnardos started its first preschool service in Dublin in 1974 — exactly 100 years after the opening of the first residential home in London. This first service was a Montessori preschool in the Children's Bus working in Sheriff Street and Rialto.

Barnardos Ireland separated from Barnardos UK in 1989 and became an independent Irish organisation. Barnardos in Ireland works with children and their families in their own communities. In conjunction with the Eastern Health Board they run a number of day nurseries. Some of these nurseries have introduced a new approach to working with young children known as the High/Scope curriculum, which will be discussed at a later stage in the text. Barnardos also have a National Children's Resource Centre incorporating information, advice and training on issues relating to children. Barnardos is located at Christ Church Place, Dublin 8.

MORE RECENT DEVELOPMENTS IN IRELAND

Irish Pre-school Playgroups Association: In 1961 a letter to *The Guardian* newspaper in England led to the establishment of one of the most flourishing associations in the field of early education. The letter was from Belle Tutaev, a mother who proposed the setting up of a playgroup so that her children would have other children to play with in a safe and stimulating environment. The result of this letter was the formation of the Pre-school Playgroup Association in England. The association emphasises the importance of play in early child development and aims to provide a rich environment in which children can meet and play. The intention was to involve parents in the education of their children by involving them in the development of the playgroups. Groups typically run for two-and-a-half to three hours each day. Through their play the children learn, in an appropriate way, about the world, its rules, its order and its joys.

In the late 1960s the idea of such a movement was being discussed in Ireland by a number of people with an interest and background in early education. The Irish Pre-school Playgroups Association (IPPA) was formed in 1969. Interest in, and membership of the association grew rapidly and the IPPA has now become an active agent in the growth of awareness about the importance and value of informal early play experiences. This organisation now provides preschool experience to over 21,000 children. Most playgroups are **home playgroups,** which people run from their own homes. Some 15% of all playgroups are **community playgroups**, which are non-profit-making and supported by a rota of mothers who work with the leader of the group. All playgroups work from the same basic philosophy and stress the value of play as a medium of learning in the early years.

The IPPA runs a wide range of courses nationwide and employ a number of region al advisors. These advisors visit playgroups and advise and support the many playgroup leaders throughout the country. The association provides guidelines for good practice, a regular newsletter and, in the absence of state registration for preschool services, offers a voluntary registration scheme for members. The IPPA is located at Inns Court, Winetavern Street, Dublin 8.

An Comhchoiste Réamhscolaíochta Teo: In the late 1960s a number of Irish-speaking playgroups were established with the support of Comhdháil Náisiúnta na

Gaeilge and Conradh na Gaeilge. These playgroups are called *naíonraí*. Many studies have shown that the earlier a language, other than the mother tongue, is introduced to a child the greater the likelihood that the learning will be retained and the greater the facility for learning other languages. This has led to the establishment of a large number of naíonraí, or Irish-speaking preschools.

In 1973 those involved in organising the naíonraí came together to form a voluntary organisation — the Naíonraí Gaelacha — under the auspices of Conradh na Gaeilge. As a result of a plan submitted by the executive board of this group to Bord na Gaeilge the Comhchoiste Réamhscoilaíochta Teo. was formed. This organisation is a joint committee of the Naíonraí Gaelacha and Bord na Gaeilge for preschooling through the medium of Irish.

An Comhchoiste now supports some 218 naíonraí catering for over 2,500 children. They are run along lines very similar to other playgroups but the language spoken is Irish. Children can attend even where their parents do not speak Irish and they are free to talk in either Irish or English. Experience has shown that most children quickly pick up the Irish language in an enjoyable and non-threatening way. The Comhchoiste have a number of regional advisors who support the naíonraí and they also provide training courses for those anxious to open a group. In addition to courses the Comhchoiste produce some basic materials for use in a naíonraí. An Comhchoiste also act as an active voice for young children. The offices of An Comhchoiste Réamhscoilaíochta Teo. are at Merrion Square, Dublin.

National Children's Nursery Association (NCNA): was formed in June 1988. Its formation follows a number of efforts during the 1980s to co-ordinate and bring together those people providing full daycare for young children and their families. The main aims of this group are:

• to provide nationwide support for those who run/work in nurseries

• to encourage the raising and maintenance of standards

• to create public awareness of the role of daycare

• to act as a pressure group in the childcare area.

To meet these aims the NCNA produce a regular newsletter and hold public meetings. They have issued a publication on good practice and are currently working on the voluntary registration of member nurseries. The NCNA can be contacted at the Carmichael Centre for Voluntary Groups, Nth Brunswick Street, Dublin.

OMEP — THE WORLD ORGANISATION FOR EARLY CHILDHOOD EDUCATION

OMEP (Organisation Mondiale pour l'Education Préscolaire) is an international non-governmental organisation affiliated to UNESCO. It was set up in 1948 to promote a greater understanding of the needs of young children and now has national committees in almost fifty countries. OMEP's primary objective has been to improve and safe-guard the welfare, education, development and happiness of all young children (0–8). OMEP in collaboration with other agencies seeks to raise awareness of young children's needs, promote good practice and initiate and support research into issues of relevance to young children and those who work with and for them. To this end OMEP will help, in so far as it can, any undertaking which could improve early childhood care and education.

The National Committee of OMEP in Ireland was founded in 1966 and since its foundation has been active in areas of relevance to the quality of life of the young child. It has acted as a meeting ground for organisations and individuals concerned with issues relating to early childhood care and education (ECCE). It has held public meetings on points of public interest and has published reports and newsletters on various topics. In the past OMEP has been supportive of developments in the field of ECCE such as the formation of the IPPA and the establishment of the National Certificate in Early Childhood Care and Education at the Dublin Institute of

Technology, Cathal Brugha Street. OMEP has also carried out research, the most recent into the establishment of a central agency for information on young children — Young Children in Ireland.

Membership of OMEP allows one to meet others with similar interests and become active in the development of policy on children and early education in Ireland.

FACTORS INFLUENCING THE DEVELOPMENT OF ECCE IN IRELAND

During the twentieth century there has been a rapid growth in the area of provision for young children throughout Europe and the US. This has happened for a wide variety of reasons and the situation in Ireland is no exception.

Early childhood care and education and the disadvantaged child: In the first place there was the recognition of the importance of early experiences to the quality of later life experiences. This was influenced by the many research studies and practical experiments in psychology and education that have been carried out, written and debated over the last fifty years.

Along with this came the growing belief that intervening in the lives of disadvantaged children at the preschool stage might improve the success of these children in their later education. This led, at first in the USA, to a growth in intervention preschool programmes known as **Headstart**. The belief underlying the Headstart programmes was that providing young disadvantaged children with experiences that were common-place for their advantaged peers would create an equality between the two groups when it came to later educational experiences. It was quite clear that disadvantaged children failed at school in much higher numbers than their advantaged peers.

The faith in simply providing preschool experiences was somewhat misplaced and many of the projects proved to be unsuccessful in achieving their ambitious aims. We now know that a lot of effort must be put into such programmes and they must be of a high quality if they are to succeed. We also know that they must include the parents as part of the whole process.

In Ireland the Department of Education and the Van Leer Foundation supported the setting up of a headstart-type programme in the late 1960s. It is still running and is known as the **Rutland Street Preschool Project**. In the early stages this project was evaluated and written up in the book *Rutland Street* by Seamus Holland. Unfortunately, it is a model that has not been established anywhere else in Ireland.

The Department of Education also provides some support for the establishment and running of preschools for travellers.

The main provision of early intervention programmes for disadvantaged young children and their families in Ireland comes through State support for voluntary organisations, often grant-aided through the Department of Health. This is an unsatisfactory situation, I believe, as it perpetuates the division of early childhood care and education services between the departments of Health and Education. This in turn can lead to delays in the development of much needed services. Furthermore, placing primary responsibility for early services with the Department of Health stresses the healthcare aspect of early childhood and not the educational. Unifying the delivery of services under the Department of Education, as has happened in Spain and New Zealand, both of which now see 0–6 as the first stage in their educational system, seems a more positive view of this period than the overlay of dependence suggested by Department of Health responsibility. This is particularly the case given the fact that a large proportion of what should be considered early educational provision is provided by the Department of Education in the non-compulsory, pre-primary, junior and senior infant classes of the primary school.

Early education is good for ALL children: A second factor in the developments in this field was the growth of interest among parents in providing stimulating play experiences for their children. This led to the establishment of the Irish Pre-school Playgroups Association (IPPA) described above and the growth in playgroups and naíonraí throughout Ireland.

This parental interest in the early experiences of their children also led to the spread of Montessori schools. Those services providing a Montessori approach for the early years emphasise the importance of the senses and use a series of well-known materials that are intended to broaden the child's ability to describe and define her world as well as expand her understanding of the world.

The changing family: A third — and now very powerful — factor in the development of early services and the need for more has been the changing structure of the family. There has been, on the one hand, a significant increase in the number of children born to and raised by lone parents and, on the other hand, a rise in the number of families where both parents work. Both these factors have led to a growth in full, private day-care provision either with childminders or nurseries. There are private and workplace nurseries, the latter area a growing one. We have, as yet, very little information about childminding in Ireland, how many childminders there are, what number of children attend or what the experiences of young children cared for in this way may be.

HOW 'CHILD-CENTRED' ARE WE?

Contemporary Western culture is considered 'child-centred' and almost everyone seems interested, to some degree, in children, their development and their welfare. When looked at more closely, however, the situation in Ireland may not be as good as it should be. In 1990 the Irish government agreed to ratify the UN Convention on the rights of the child. This convention is intended to secure the rights of all children globally and move towards a world where we will not see young children starve or die from want of simple medication. It is intended to protect children from violence and war and poverty. The government ratified the convention in September 1992. It is now essential that this convention be made more public so that we can judge how well we meet the needs and rights of our children.

In Ireland we may appear to be fond of children but when we look at policy as a measure of our commitment and interest the situation is not as good as it might be. For instance, and this is important particularly with regard to children who are at risk or in need of protection, the Child Care Act was signed into law in July 1991. At the time of writing only a few sections of this large Act are operational and there is very little funding available to resource the whole Act. The Department of Education, in the Green Paper — *Education for a Changing World*, also recognises the importance of preschool provision, particularly to children at risk of educational disadvantage. This paper states that, when resources are available, there will be an expansion of preschool services to this population.

There are a large number of children in poverty in Ireland. Although there are many projects and innovations from within the voluntary sector to overcome this problem there is no coherent national policy on children, in general, and child poverty in particular. These factors and others must be borne in mind when studying the situation of early childhood care and education in Ireland.

In any book concerned with the care and education of young children due consideration must also be given to the role of the family, community and society in general. Recent social, economic and political trends have impacted on local communities affecting the structure and nature of families, the role of women and the lives of children. By its nature this book will deal with factors affecting the child in a segmented way and the fuller picture of influence and effect, interaction and influence must not be lost sight of. With the changes that are occurring — not only in our society but in the world in general — we need adults to be sensitive to the needs of children. We also need a variety of well-developed early childhood services provided by well-trained staff to meet the varied needs of children and their families. This book is intended as an introduction to early childhood care and education and as a starter for all those who wish to take on the responsibility of working with and for young children.

SUMMARY

The importance of childhood as a period of development began to emerge in the seventeenth century. Prior to this, children were seen as little adults and treated with scant regard for their developmental needs. Philosophers such as Locke and Rousseau and educators such as Pestalozzi, Froebel and Montessori were all influential in raising the awareness of the importance of early experiences to later development.

As a result of the many changes following the Industrial Revolution much social legislation was brought in to ensure adequate protection and education of young children. Not all their experiences were of the best sort but by the turn of the century children were recognised as active agents in their development and efforts were made to provide them with early experiences which would enhance rather than inhibit their development.

Along with the growth of interest among those working in the field of child development parents were becoming more aware of the needs of their children and forming an influential group to act as a pressure for the development of early services. This can be seen in Ireland with the growth over the last thirty years in preschools, playgroups, naíonraí and day nurseries.

As the century draws to a close other social changes — such as the rise in lone parent families and homes where both parents work — will lead to further developments in the field of early childhood care and education.

EXERCISES

1. What is meant by the term **zeitgeist**?

2. In what way did the work of Locke and Rousseau alter the earlier view of childhood?

3. Whose work led to the development of **observation** as a widely used method of child study?

4. Maria Montessori was a doctor with a special interest in the education of young children. What did she mean by a 'planned' environment?

5. Discuss with a partner the meaning of the term 'child-centred'.

6. Name any book you have read that describes a childhood from another age.

7. List four games you played as a young child. Can you list any games young children are playing now that you **did not** play?

8. How did Froebel's view of education and play influence our current practice in early education and care?

9. List the different forms of preschool education available to young children in Ireland.

10. Find out what you can about **one** of the following:

   - The IPPA

   - An Comhchoiste Réamhscoilaíochta Teo.

   - The NCNA

   - The St Nicholas Montessori Society, Ireland

   - OMEP

chapter 2
working with children

It is generally agreed that children need to feel loved, respected and listened to. They are sociable and enjoy the company of other children and adults, even when very young. They learn their skills, acquire their knowledge, develop their concepts and their attitudes through contact with others and they do so best when they meet with affection, positive social interaction and a stimulating environment. There have been many examples of the way in which severe deprivation in these aspects of life has led to serious delay and impairment in the development of children.

Childcare and early education should aim to ensure that children experience a healthy and safe environment that respects the child and encourages self-confidence and an interest in learning. Adults should strive to provide a stable learning and caring environment that allows for spontaneous expression and fosters sociability, friendship and co-operation with others. This should be provided in collaboration with family and community. The early childhood worker must also be able to communicate with and empathise with individual parents. Recognising the importance of truly sharing the care of children that is involved in all early services is important if these services are to prove valuable to children. These may appear to be ambitious aims but it is difficult to expect anyone providing early childhood services to aim for less.

The early childhood worker must be able to deal with young children in a sympathetic manner, handling carefully their early social and emotional development, guiding their cognitive awareness and stimulating their physical accomplishments. She must be able to provide for the child in the context of now and not in terms of the notion that she is providing something that is only preparatory to something else. This important point was addressed by the French philosopher J. J. Rousseau in the eighteenth century when he wrote 'Nature wants children to be children before they are men. If we deliberately pervert this order, we shall get premature fruits which are neither ripe nor well flavoured and will soon decay.' This focus on meeting the needs and desires of the child for the value it has *now* is something that adults may find difficult.

ADULTS AND CHILDREN WORKING TOGETHER

We have all been children but that does not mean that we all understand children. Indeed, we have a tendency to think of children in terms of adult thinking and behaviour and this can give us an inaccurate view of the child. From observation and studies of children over the years, particularly over the last fifty years, we are now in a position to make statements about children, the way they develop and their needs. From this we can plan to improve the quality of life for young children, particularly those children who are at a disadvantage, whatever the reason.

Children are different: The rate at which children develop through their lives varies from child to child and depends on factors such as inherited potential, environmental experiences and personal history. They show strength and weaknesses in different areas and at different times. But . . .

Children are the same: They follow the same pattern of development as they grow from infants to adults. These patterns are easily identified in language and physical development. We know they are also present in the less visible areas of development such as thinking and social development.

Children need adults: This is particularly true in their early years but we must not lose sight of the fact that we need children too. Learning about children from theory is of little value on its own. To understand children we must experience them. Every relationship is interactive; individuals affect each other. In any social interaction there is a system at work. Within a system the various elements affect each other.

This system can be simply described in the following diagram:

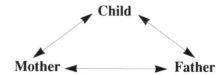

Here you can see the interactive effect. In this example there is equal interaction between the members; in a dysfunctioning system, however, this would not be the case. One or other of the elements would dominate and this would affect the working of the whole system. Where, for instance, the father is generally absent, the balance between the child and the mother and that between the child and the father would have a different value.

This dynamic is present even where the system is made complex by the presence of a wide number of individuals — such as a preschool group of eight children and two adults or in a family group. That the systems at work here are complex should not lead us to ignore them. In looking at a system of which one is a part it is difficult to judge the influences. To be aware that there are such influences will, however, assist in recognising them.

UNDERSTANDING CHILDREN

For adults to work effectively with children it is important to understand them. This is best approached by careful child study and self-analysis. Respecting the child requires that we take children seriously, observe and interpret what they do and take what they say seriously. There is no doubt that it can be irritating when a child repeatedly asks the same question. Instead of becoming irritated, however, it is useful to ask yourself why they repeatedly ask the question — to take their intention seriously and try to understand it. For example it might be that they do not understand your answer, or that your answer only raises another aspect of the question. It may be that they feel you are not attending to them when you reply and their repetition is an attempt to gain your attention — here it may be the attention rather than the answer that is important.

In observing and listening to children we must try to understand the meaning of what they do or say. Often the meaning may depend on our understanding of child development and the child's own individuality. By recognising what the child's behaviour means we can use this as a base for moving on in our work with the child. For instance, a three-year-old child who is playing with water and fills and empties the same vessel a number of times, is not merely playing with water but is experiencing water and experiencing what full and empty means. By providing a selection of vessels in the water tray we can allow the child to broaden this experience to 'half full', 'twice as full' and so on. This is, of course, done without expecting them to understand the more abstract concepts of 'half full' or 'twice as full'.

ADULTS: INFLUENCES AND LIMITATIONS

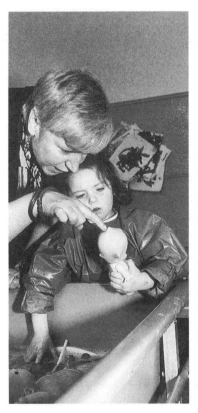

While it is acknowledged that adults are hugely influential in the lives of children it should also be recognised that there are limitations to our influence. These limitations are set by factors within the child, by the circumstances of our involvement with the child and by the power of influence of outside factors. For example, while we can work hard to ensure the quality of life for a young child who is blind, we cannot entirely overcome the effect of that blindness on the development of the child. Similarly we may have some impact on the quality of a child's life in the context of a good quality nursery service, but the effectiveness of that influence will be tempered by the child's family experiences and how the family rate the importance of nursery provision. If the home environment is disorganised it may be difficult to be as effective as one would wish.

To help us understand the meaning behind children's actions and words it is helpful also to try and speak to children in a way that will help them understand us: to ground our conversation in the real world rather than speaking in the abstract; to be clear and simple in what we say. Adult influence can be good or poor for the child. Below is a table to illustrate this point.

Good Adult Influence	Poor Adult Influence
Adults as a positive model of behaviour	Adults as a negative model
Adults using power in a positive way	Adults abusing their power
Adults who empower children	Adults who control children
Adults who stimulate children	Adults who direct children
Adults who listen	Adults who tell
Adults who protect	Adults who over-protect
Adults who are consistent	Adults who are inconsistent

Some of the points outlined above may appear very obvious but it is surprising how negative our effect on children can be over time — often reflecting the way in which we experienced childhood ourselves.

Take the issue of **modelling appropriate behaviour**. If we want children to listen, for instance, we must model appropriate listening behaviour. If we want children to speak quietly we must not shout our wishes across a room but we must model appropriate behaviour by speaking quietly. Where you expect children to wear aprons at 'messy' activities you should also endeavour to wear aprons, where appropriate.

In relation to **positive and negative power** this refers to the manner in which children's behaviour is regulated or controlled. All children benefit from knowing what the rules are and in being rewarded for good behaviour. Good and Bad are based on value judgments and it is important that all adults have a broadly similar idea of what is meant. If your approach to children's 'misbehaviour' is to reprimand them and tell them to behave 'because I say so' you are controlling their behaviour without helping them understand why certain behaviour is not allowed and other behaviour is accepted and desired. It is inappropriate to consider a young child wrong if they will not share a particular toy — the ability to share is difficult to acquire and will take time. This does not mean that you don't encourage sharing but it is essential to be realistic and positive rather than unrealistic and negative with children.

When working with young children outside their home or as a childminder within their home you are sharing the care of children. This should be done in collaboration with parents as far as is possible. This is important because, if for no other reason, it allows for an increased likelihood of consistency in the way the child is treated. This is crucial if the child is to have a sense of security and stability so essential for positive personal development.

FINDING OUT ABOUT CHILDREN

In approaching the study of children and child development there are a variety of different perspectives that researchers can take. These perspectives or approaches to study are not mutually exclusive — rather they focus on a different aspect of the complex phenomenon that is child development. There is no 'right' or 'wrong' approach to the study of child development, but it is important to be aware of the different approaches, as they may yield apparently conflicting explanations for the same behaviour. This reflects the differences in their focus and is similar to two pictures of the same object taken at different angles. Both pictures are depicting the same object but the outcome is completely different.

APPROACHES TO THE STUDY OF BEHAVIOUR

For our purpose there are three main approaches to the study of child development. These are :

* The Behaviourist approach

* The Cognitive Developmental approach

* The Psychodynamic approach

It is valuable to be aware of their different focus as this allows you to evaluate the points made. When presented with a behaviour you need to explain you may find that one approach rather than another suits the particular situation. A different approach to the study of children may lead to a different way of dealing with a problem. For instance:

> . . . a child of two years suddenly starts to bite other children. Dealing with this behaviour can be approached by observing the child, noting the number of times she bites, noting who she bites, identifying factors that elicit or cause the behaviour and those factors that maintain the behaviour. Armed with this information the adult might alter certain elements in the child's environment, such as ensuring that the child who bites is closely watched when a possible victim is nearby to decrease the opportunity for biting or the adult might reward alternative behaviours particularly those that are incompatible with biting. This method of addressing the situation draws on the Behaviourist approach.
>
> From the Psychodynamic perspective the behaviour would be seen as a sign of an underlying difficulty. One would look to the child's experiences and assess to what degree there had been any change that might account for the biting or you might attempt to identify if there was a problem that the child was trying to cope with. This could be done by watching her play, looking at her art work which may yield clues as to what is upsetting her.

The Behaviourist Approach: This approach derives from the work of **J. B. Watson** (1878–1958). He believed that Locke was correct in considering all babies as *tabula rasa* — that is, born with a mind like a blank slate, waiting to be written on. He argued that psychology — the study of behaviour — needed to become scientific and that any behaviour that was to be fully understood must be observable and measurable. The method recommended was to study what people do and to try and understand the factors that cause them to behave in a particular way. Watson helped shape the course of psychology over the early part of this century.

B.F. Skinner (1904–1989), following the lead of Watson, became particularly interested in those factors that cause behaviour to occur, what maintains behaviour and how it can, when considered inappropriate or maladaptive, be eliminated.

His approach to understanding behaviour involved careful study of three factors and can be seen in terms of the **ABC** model:

* the Antecedents (what causes the behaviour)

* the Behaviour itself

* the Consequences of the behaviour.

Skinner's work has had a significant influence in the area of education with regard to planning activities and experiences, classroom management and classroom control. It has also influenced practice in clinical work in terms of behaviour modification procedures where one plans carefully to increase appropriate behaviour and decrease inappropriate behaviour.

The Cognitive/Developmental Approach: Cognition refers to the mental processes of perception, memory and information processing necessary to acquiring knowledge and to reasoning about and solving problems. Cognitive psychology is the study of these processes with a view to developing a theory of how they work. The cognitive approach to the study of child development is concerned with the way in which development emerges and how behaviour is influenced by the cognitive level of the individual. Cognitive psychologists do not consider that the individual is a *tabula rasa*. Rather they consider that the human mind actively processes the information it receives and comes equipped to do so at birth.

Perhaps the most influential individual in the field of modern studies of child development was **Jean Piaget** (1896–1980). His view of cognitive development has had a profound influence on both psychological and educational theory and practice over the last thirty to forty years. His cognitive/developmental approach has stimulated research, some of which is now leading to a re-evaluation of his original theory. His theory focused attention on the child's active involvement in her own learning and fostered the practice of a more child-centred approach to working with children. In relation to early childhood education his work supports the belief that play is a valuable way for children to learn and emphasises the need for activities to be appropriate to the developmental level of the child; that is, not too advanced or, indeed, too simple. His work will be discussed in greater detail later in the text.

The Psychodynamic Approach: This approach was developed by **Sigmund Freud** (1856–1939). The basic assumption underlying Freud's view was that our behaviour stems from and is influenced by our unconscious; that is, by the fears and desires within us, of which we are unaware. To understand why we behave as we do it is necessary to gain access to this unconscious and to try to unravel its mysteries. His work

has been mainly influential in the clinical field, particularly in the treatment of children with emotional problems. The use of Play Therapy with young, troubled children as a means of communicating with them has emerged from the psychodynamic tradition.

RESEARCH METHODS

In reading the results of any piece of work it is helpful to be aware of the approach used by the authors. It is also necessary to understand what type of research method was used, what sample size and type. This is important because it allows us to weigh up the value of any particular study. Often it is the headline that catches our attention and stays in our memory but the headline may not be a true reflection of the piece of work reported and may, in fact, be misleading. Each research design has its advantages and disadvantages. I will describe six types of research design: longitudinal studies, cross-sectional studies, tests, survey/interview, observation and experiment.

Longitudinal studies: These study the same sample of people over a given period of time, every seven years, for example. It is valuable as it shows a sequential pattern of events and the developmental progress of individuals. It has disadvantages, however, including the expense, the time commitment and the fact that subjects in the sample may fall away. Two important longitudinal studies mentioned in this book are the 'New York Longitudinal Study' and the 'Perry Preschool High/Scope Project'.

Cross-sectional studies: Using this method different samples of people at different ages are all studied at the same time. You might study a group of seven, fourteen and twenty-one-year-olds all at the same time rather than choose a group and study them first at seven, then at fourteen and finally at twenty-one — the case with longitudinal studies. This method has the advantage of being less time-consuming and expensive. It yields a picture of average developmental change but cannot allow for the effect of different, time-related variables and does not allow for any interpretation regarding individual development.

Tests: These are standardised tests developed by researchers to assess different aspects of behaviour. The most commonly known tests are *intelligence tests* which yield a measure of a person's intellectual level or IQ (Intelligence Quotient), *aptitude tests* which identify areas of strength in an individual and *personality tests* which attempt to identify different personality traits. You may have had some experience of these tests during your school years. Using data from standardised tests different individuals can be compared and individual performance can be measured against the norm, that is, for example, the expected performance for an individual of a particular age. However, these tests are limited in that only predetermined responses can be accepted and they may not allow for particular cultural or linguistic characteristics.

Survey/interview: This is often a quick way to get information about attitudes, opinions or behaviour but it is problematic as questions may be ambiguous or they may be leading, that is they may unintentionally direct the responder to answer in a particular way. Also it is a feature of human nature that people answer questions in the way they think they *should* which does not always reflect the true situation.

Observation: This is a technique that is widely used in the study of child development. Observation can be either *structured* or *naturalistic*.

- Structured observation is where behaviour is observed in a standard situation, such as a laboratory playroom. Data from different subjects can be compared and there is no predetermined response. However, behaviour observed may not generalise to the real world, that is the observed behaviour may be specific to the environment in which it is observed and may not be a representation of typical behaviour.

- Naturalistic observation is where spontaneous behaviour is observed in a familiar environment such as the home or a nursery. In working with young children there is a great deal of opportunity to use this method and it is a valuable skill to develop. The advantages are that this procedure yields information about behaviour in the real world and allows for the detailed description of what a child can actually do in different situations. The disadvantages are that it does not assess maximum performance because, unlike a test, the observer is not posing problems. Also, because there are no requests for particular behaviours it is possible that certain abilities will not be observed and you cannot assume that the child does or does not have them in her repertoire.

Experiment: An experiment is planned and carried out with a random sample of individuals. It allows for the responses of different groups — such as boys/girls, young/old — to be compared. It also allows for the comparison of individual performances to be measured against a norm, as in standardised tests. However, as the experiment is usually laboratory or clinic based it is difficult to generalise results to the real world.

There are many other research designs and I would suggest that before you quote a 'well-known fact', you are sure that you are aware of the strengths and weaknesses of the design employed. The table below summarises the types of research design and the advantages and disadvantages of each:

ADVANTAGES AND DISADVANTAGES OF DIFFERENT RESEARCH DESIGNS AND METHODS

Design & Method	Advantages	Disadvantages
Longitudinal Studies	Show developmental curves for individuals and groups. Show the effect of time.	Expensive, time-consuming. Subjects may drop out over duration of the study.
Cross-sectional Studies	Give a view of average developmental change with age.	Do not indicate individual growth curves or the effect of time.
Tests	Data from different people can be compared to each other and to a norm.	Data limited to a set of given responses.
Survey/Interview	Quick way to get details. Only way to assess attitudes and intentions.	Interviewees are biased and inaccurate reporters of past events.
Observation (Structured)	Data from different people can be compared. Data not restricted to a given set of responses.	Does not assess underlying attitudes. Not possible to assume that observed responses will occur elsewhere.
Observation (Naturalistic)	Provides information about behaviour in the real world.	Settings for different people are not comparable. Cannot assess all possible behaviour.
Experiment	Gives group differences related to conditions such as socio-economic status or sex.	Subjects may be different in ways other than those of interest to the researchers.

SUMMARY

Children and adults affect each other. While the power of adults is very great there are limitations.

The study of children has been of interest to many over the centuries. Different approaches to studying children can yield different information. When reading about children and their behaviour and needs it is important to be aware of the approach and the design of the study used by the authors. The three models of psychology discussed in this section are: the Behaviourist, Cognitive/ Developmental and Psychodynamic models. In studying children and their behaviour, different research designs can be used. Each design has advantages and disadvantages.

EXERCISES

1. Identify the factors that may limit the influence of an adult on a child.

2. List and briefly describe the three approaches to the study of behaviour outlined in this chapter.

3. What is the difference between a longitudinal and a cross-sectional study?

4. Outline the advantages and disadvantages of the survey/interview technique.

5. What is meant by the following:

   • Norm

   • Naturalistic Observation

   • *Tabula Rasa.*

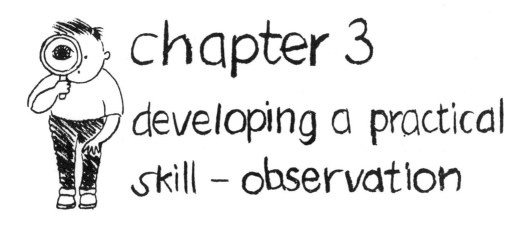

chapter 3
developing a practical skill – observation

OBSERVATION

To work effectively and successfully with children you must know and understand them. Studying child development is a basic requirement for working with children but it is of little value if you cannot apply what you learn in theory to the reality of the practical situation. Developing the skill of observing children and interpreting what you observe by reference to your knowledge is essential to this task. Personal experience of children — derived from practical placement work as a student and everyday exposure when working with children — is enhanced when skilled observation is used. It is by closely observing behaviour that you come to understand the theoretical information derived from research studies into children and their development. Knowing about child development is one thing — being able to interpret the individual child and her behaviour in a helpful way to you both is something else. Knowing and understanding are not the same thing and it is understanding that is required if you are to enrich children — your own or those of others — by your contact with them. The individual needs and abilities of children, their uniqueness — even in a group — is only accessible through careful observation.

BEING OBJECTIVE

The single most important thing about information acquired through observation is that it should be objective. That is, it should represent exactly what is observed with no personal or subjective interpretation. If, when caring for a three-year-old, you are kicked by her, interpreting this behaviour in the light of your theoretical knowledge and your knowledge of the particular child may help you understand the reason for the behaviour. This will allow you to help the child over the difficulty rather than becoming angry with the child as if the kick were a personal attack.

As a species we are equipped with a wide variety of receptors with which to observe the world. We sense through the eyes, ears, mouth, nose and skin. Yet, if we were to respond to all the information that we acquire through observation without, in some way making judgments about the relative importance of the observed material we would spend so much time observing and reacting that we would achieve very little. As a result we have a very finely-tuned and well-developed sense of observation and it is subjective. We *observe, interpret quickly* and *react (or ignore)*. Take, for instance, crossing a busy road. We stand at the kerb, look in the direction of oncoming traffic and make judgments about the distance of the car, its relative speed and our ability to cross in safety. We observe the traffic, we calculate and interpret on the basis of our observations and we react by crossing the road or not. We don't, however, carefully note the colour and make of each car, or the registration numbers or the number of motorbikes. This is all observed but deemed irrelevant to the task in hand. In other words our observations are selective and subjective. We decide what is important or relevant to the particular situation.

For **objective** observation we must adjust our natural tendency to select particular aspects and reject others. We need to insert a new step in the previously outlined pattern. Thus in objective observations we *observe, record, interpret* and *react (or ignore)*. This inserted step of *record* is necessary as it forces us to look closely at what we actually see. Initially the recording must be done manually, by writing down clearly and explicitly what is observed and only what is observed. As you become more experienced and practised it is a skill that you can call on at any time. With practice and over time the objectivity of your observations comes without the necessity of immediate, accurate recording. This skill is acquired more slowly than you might expect.

Observers may be inclined to be interpretive; to observe a situation and weave a story or explanation around the facts. For research purposes it is necessary to develop the skill of objective observation and leave interpreting until later on. It is difficult to record objectively but with practice one can switch into the objective mode when seeking to explain or understand a particular child's behaviour. It is from my own practical experience that I can appreciate how difficult it can be and urge you to take seriously the development of the skill. If you do not observe clearly and objectively, your observations will be little more than opinions and may even perpetuate myths rather than explain situations. To illustrate what I mean let me tell a story:

On a visit to a children's centre some time ago I was speaking to a member of staff. Behind me, on the wall, was a full-length mirror. Through this I could clearly see the children in the room. There was a movement session in progress. The staff member to whom I was speaking was facing into the room. After some time a dispute arose between a small number of children. The staff member excused herself and went to the group. She removed one little girl and asked her to wait by the wall.

When she returned she explained that this particular girl, like her brothers and sisters before her, was a giddy child always causing trouble. As it happens I had seen the disturbance, through the mirror, and it was a different child who had started the dispute. The accused little girl, though a party to the problem, was not the main player. Her presence in the group, however, and the history she brought with her, made it easy for the staff member to assume — without actually seeing — that she was the cause of the disruption. While not denying that the child might indeed be difficult, a more objective observation of the circumstances would not have led to the outcome I observed and would have been fairer to the young girl in question.

Too often we cloud our observations by our expectations; we interpret on the basis of what we think rather than what we really observe.

PREPARING FOR OBSERVATION

Practice is a key factor in the development of the skill of objective observation. Set yourself some tasks; for example, observe a child at water play for five minutes, record the routine at lunch-time by focusing on one particular child, observe a group of children at outdoor play for a ten minute period or observe and record the language interaction between two children in the 'home corner' or while at imaginative play. Such exercises help you assess your own progress at observing and at the same time give you useful information about the children, the routine and the activities. When recording, endeavour to separate fact from interpretation; write 'she had a smile on her face' rather than 'she was happy'. This latter statement is an interpretation of what you actually see. Also be specific in what you record — when focusing on a particular child ensure that you remain attending to that child. It may also be necessary to adjust your style to the recording needs of the situation. There are some points to bear in mind before you embark on these exercises.

Time: Observation initially takes longer than expected. To gather a useful five-minute record, for example, could take up to fifteen minutes. As you begin there is a settling-in period. This is an important time as you want to establish yourself as unobtrusively as possible so that your presence affects the child's behaviour as little as possible. Once settled you can begin to record the activity over the five minute period. Following this you will need a short wind-down time to record, briefly, what, if anything, happened next. As the skill develops, the amount of time necessary for each exercise decreases but a five minute record will, generally, take up to ten minutes to complete. It is also important to decide what timing scale you will use in recording your observations. Will you look for half a minute and then record or will you look at all times and write as you see? Different record schedules will be discussed below.

Planning: What to observe is the first question you must ask yourself. It is not enough simply to decide to observe children. Try it, there is so much to see that you could not possibly record a worthwhile cross-section. It is necessary, in the beginning, to select one child and only observe her behaviour, excluding language content. You will find that it is difficult to observe and write down what you see and continue to observe all at the same time. Indeed your first records will contain gaps in the time span where, although you have no record of what happened, the child was engaged in some activity — even staring into space.

It is useful to have the page on which you will write your observations prepared before you begin. This can save a lot of time during the actual exercise. A useful record schedule was that devised by Kathy Sylva and her colleagues in the Oxford Preschool Project. The background to her method and the schedule is well documented in her book *Childwatching at Playgroup and Nursery School*. For their research they chose to observe only one child — the Target Child — at a time. I use a shortened version (see below) of their record sheet for early practice observations with my students and find it very satisfactory.

On the record sheet at the top there is space for your name, details about the child (age, sex) and details of the setting and time of the observation. You will notice that there is no section for the name of the child. This is to maintain confidentiality: it is not necessary for the name to be recorded in practice observations.

SAMPLE RECORD SHEET:*

Name of observer: _____

Age of child: _____   Sex of child: _____

Date of observation: _____   Time of observation: _____

Setting: _____
_____
_____

MINUTES	ACTIVITY	LANGUAGE	SOCIAL SETTING
0.00			
0.05			
1.00			

43

*Adapted from Sylva, K. *et al*, *Childwatching at playgroup and nursery school* (Grant McIntyre, London 1980)

Underneath the introductory section you will see four columns marked out; these are used as follows:

- **Minutes:** This column is for recording the time of the observations recorded. In this schedule an observation is recorded every half minute. There are, therefore, ten time sections for a five minute record. Each time section, 0.00, 0.50, 1.00, 1.50, 2.00 minutes and so on, should be the same size. This is important as it allows you to observe if there is a pattern of a lot of activity or very little in a half minute period.

- **Activity:** The second column is for recording the behaviour observed. Here you write exactly what you see. If there is a word that you cannot think of leave it blank and continue to write. The object of the exercise is to gather a continuous record of behaviour so that all of the five minute period is recorded on the sheet. In recording activity you will find that a great deal can happen in a half minute. It is useful, therefore, to develop a shorthand such as 'TC holding crayon in RH, Moves to LH, Makes marks on the paper'. This indicates that the child is holding the crayon in her right hand, transfers it to her left hand and then makes a mark on the paper. Try to state what you see as simply as possible. You must avoid recording what you think the child is doing or feeling and you must not guess at the motivation for the behaviour or the emotion.

To illustrate:

- **Sarah was delighted to see her mother**

- **Sarah jumped up from the table and ran, smiling, to her mother**

In the first of these records there is inference and interpretation. What does 'delighted' really mean, how is it defined? There is room for confusion and mistakes. In the second record there is a simple, clear statement of the observed behaviour and one can interpret the emotion more clearly. In this example it is probably safe to assume that the interpretation is accurate but this cannot always be assumed. It is the style of the latter record that is recommended as a truly objective and useful record.

When writing down what you observe it is important to continue observing what you began observing. This may sound very obvious and simple but I have found that, initially, students begin to observe the behaviour of TC. During the course of the observation the TC interacts with another child, C, and for a period of the observation it is the behaviour of C that is recorded in place of that of TC.

When writing down what you observe take care not to write anything you would not be willing to share with others or anything you are not prepared to stand over. This does not mean that you never record examples of anti-social behaviour or activities that failed to work out as expected. Often how you phrase a point observed is what counts. For instance, writing 'She tugged at mother's skirt. TC called mother and tugged at skirt again — TC begins to cry' is a much clearer and non-judgmental way of recording an episode than 'TC tried to show mother her picture but mother was chatting to staff and ignored her. TC got into a rage'.

- **Language:** In the third column you can record language interaction. When focusing on behaviour in general it is of little value to try and record language content as well. Indeed observing and recording the content of language interactions is a highly complex and technically difficult exercise. For the purpose of training observations it is sufficient to record a language event. This is done on this schedule by using a shorthand where the Target Child is referred to as TC, any other child is recorded as C and any adult as A. Thus the recorded interaction A–TC, TC–A is an exchange between an adult and the target child initiated by the adult and responded to by the child. This type of shorthand is very valuable for observing conversation flows, the intensity of language interaction and the level of adult versus child-initiated exchanges. It cannot, however, be used to evaluate the complexity of the language as there is no record of content.

- **Social setting:** The fourth and final column is for recording the social setting in which the observed behaviour occurred. It can be quite brief, for example: 'TC at table, three other children at table. Table holds paste, paper of various colours, brushes and each child has a large sheet of paper. Adult is moving from table to table. One other adult is supervising water play'. As your record progresses you might want to include a setting comment to account for an observed behaviour in the target child. For instance, 'TC's mother enters the room' could account for the observation that 'TC left the table and moved towards the door'. If the setting information is not included then one might assume that the TC was lacking in concentration or bored or aimlessly moving around. This type of precision in recording may appear tedious but good observation skill is so essential an aspect of good quality practice that careful training in the area is essential.

Section of a completed record

SAMPLE RECORD SHEET:

Name of observer: _Nóirín Hayes_

Age of child: _3 yrs 2 mths_   Sex of child: _Male_

Date of observation: _21-12-93_   Time of observation: _11-00 am_

Setting: _Boy with green and white jumper has just gone to the table having said blue is his favourite colour. Stands and eats at the table._

MINUTES	ACTIVITY	LANGUAGE	SOCIAL SETTING
0.00	Holds mouth wide open and squeals. Sits down and takes bread. Looks at adult and takes a bite of bread.	TC →	
0.05	Chews open mouth and makes noises. Picks up bread – stands up – walks to A and gives A a crust. Stands and watches A as she peels an orange. Runs to table, makes a face and	TC → TC → A	
1.00			

47

INTERPRETING YOUR RECORD

Having completed the observation it is important — indeed essential — that you re-read what is written and synthesise or analyse the observation in terms of what you know about child development in general and the child and context observed in particular. In this way, points of importance can be noted and acted on. Let us take an example. You have been asked to carry out a five minute observation of a child at sand play (once selected it does not matter if the child moves from sand to another activity). You choose Louise who is three-and-a-half years old. On re-reading your record you notice that over the five minutes recorded Louise has spoken to no child and has not been addressed by any child. Is this an important observation? Well, you know that, developmentally, the average three-and-a-half- year-old has good conversation, some errors of grammar and pronunciation but generally good linguistic competence. You also know that social play and interactive play are characteristics of this age although sharing may be difficult at times. Was your observation carried out while Louise was concentrating on a particular activity? Is she generally a child who does not talk or was this an unusual occurrence? You may now need to carry out further observations to answer these questions. From these you have more detail and, let us say, Louise has not been observed talking to any children. This now poses other questions such as: is she happy at the moment, has she been neglected recently, is she sad, has she a hearing loss, is she developmentally delayed and so on. The results of these further obser-vations will allow you to respond to her needs as appropriate, within the daycare setting or calling on other professionals, as necessary.

EXERCISE*

Working with a partner, write down the ages at which you think children should be able to do the following and compare your results with another pair:

* Say 'please' and 'thank you' _____

* Be toilet-trained _____

* Know their letters _____

* Recite a rhyme _____

* Pour their own juice _____

* Ride a tricycle _____

* Use a scissors _____

*Adapted from M. J. Drummond, & D. Rouse, *Making Assessment Work* (NCB, London, 1992).

Many adults, parents and professionals, are inclined to compare children and assess the development of individual children against the perceived norm, or expected behaviour for the age group. Through observation of children we learn that there are wide variations between 'normal' children in terms of growth, development and achievement. A tall, talkative but socially immature four-year-old may be just as normal as a small, quiet, socially mature four-year-old. Children of the same age may be different and may appear more advanced in one area of development and less in another: these differences are not necessarily a cause for concern but adults may overestimate or underestimate what children of different ages can do.

Observing and recording children's behaviour is not the same as testing them. It is not intended as a test of what they can do but a guide to you as to how you can stimulate and interest them. Observations made in familiar, everyday settings can be extremely valuable. Indeed working with children on a regular basis and observing them objectively over time may give a clearer sense of the progress of development than a formal assessment, where a child may be anxious, off form or unsettled. Working regularly with a child you see her at different times of the day under varied circumstances and this may be helpful in discussing developmental progress with a parent or other professional.

Observing children to understand them better is particularly valuable with younger children, who are not always able to tell you what it is they want or what is causing them to be happy or sad. For instance, three-year-old Katie is tearful and clingy and needs more comforting than usual. Because you understand about the factors influencing the behaviour of young children and are aware of Katie's particular situation (her mother is away for some days and it is typical of a child of Katie's age and temperament to miss her and to express this in the behaviour described) you can meet her needs. All this knowledge allows you to respond appropriately whereas in an adult with less sensitivity to child development Katie may receive a quick hug and the advice to 'be a big girl now, you're not a baby'.

John is two and increasingly to be found in arguments and squabbles over activities and toys. Recognising his growing independence and his testing of the idea 'I don't want to', allows you to deal with him sympathetically and effectively rather than becoming irritable and punitive. This does not mean that you do not require a certain standard of behaviour but it is more likely that you understand what is at work when you understand the progress of child development.

WHY SHOULD WE OBSERVE?

The prime purpose of observing children is to improve our understanding of them and of their abilities and needs in order to help them as best we can. Observations are not made as a means of passing judgment on a child or of comparing one child with another. Hasty judgments are to be avoided — while opportunities for observation present themselves frequently, good quality, informative observations are not that simple to achieve.

After all, if we like children and make sure they are safe and happy, what more do they need? The responsibility of caring for children is often underrated. It is essential that its true worth be recognised and this can best be achieved by a truly professional approach to the job. This does not require that you wear a uniform and behave in a particular way — it requires that you recognise the importance of the job in hand and give it the attention it deserves.

Working with children requires that you understand them, ensure their health and safety, provide for their full development on a variety of levels, encourage them, praise them, provide materials and space. Furthermore, it demands that you recognise their needs as they arise, pick up on any areas of concern and challenge where appropriate. Working with children involves interacting with them by being there, listening, talking, assessing and watching. It does not involve planning everything they do from the moment you meet them or fitting them into your routine and personal agenda.

OBSERVATION ALLOWS YOU TO

- Observe a new placement and get a feel for the routine, accurately locate the position of the first aid kit, the fire extinguisher and so on.

- Understand a particular child — her hand/eye co-ordination, her social skills, her conversational ability, colour recognition, food likes and dislikes, her sleep pattern and toilet pattern. At any time in working with children you should be able to say: 'I know Clare can thread spools but she is only developing the skill of bead threading', or 'Ali recognises blue and red but is still unsure about the other primary colours', or 'Stephen is still a little poor on toileting routine'.

- Evaluate your own work: 'Is that activity too easy for Laura, she seems to be doing it in a repetitive fashion' or 'Could I provide a better dressing-up selection, David and Fiona seem to need more hospital-like material for their games'. Observing children helps you focus on your style of interacting. Do you encourage conversation between children or are you inclined to seek silence? Are the activities adult-directed or do you let children experiment? Does your relaxed style encourage chaos or a busy, constructive and happy atmosphere?

- Evaluate the daily routine: if Darren is unsteady in his running does he need to be outside more? Are the children irritable because they are bored or not given enough time to complete their activities? Have you changed the routine recently? Are you expecting too much, too little from the children? How can you tell?

- Plan for change: knowing the pattern of development and knowing the children allows you plan for a developmentally appropriate sequence of activities.

OBSERVE REGULARLY

To collect details that will be of value in planning and evaluating your work in the context of the children is important. It is not, however, sufficient to simply record observations every now and then and leave it at that — you must record at reasonably regular intervals and you must evaluate and interpret what you record in terms of your theoretical knowledge and specific knowledge of the children observed.

Observation on a regular basis is particularly important if you are working with young children who may have special needs or if you are likely to be called on to advise about the development of children with whom you work. Through observing social interaction, play, response to adults, to stress and general functioning you can give accurate and detailed information on individual children as required. For this data to be of value it must be clearly stated, objective and non-judgmental. You are, of course, free to offer your opinion on the report but the more objective the actual report the greater its value in the long run.

OBSERVATION TECHNIQUES

Observation as a technique in child study goes back to the earliest studies of this century. It was through close observation and recording that Gesell and Piaget, for instance, gathered their material. Certain of the early observations have been criticised for the subjectivity of the records but the techniques have been refined over the years and observation is now considered an important source of useful material in the study of development. Many different techniques have been developed with influence from different schools of thought but they can be broken down into four main approaches.

Naturalistic	**Clinical setting**
Participatory(A)	Participatory(B)
Non-participatory(C)	Non-participatory(D)

To take each of the above options separately:

A. Participatory observation in a natural setting refers to the daily observations made by those who work with young children as they- work with them. While reading them a story you would observe the contribution of different children. You would note various facts such as the level of comprehension, the articulation of sounds, the level of concentration, interest, the complexity of questions, the accuracy of answers and so on. You are not testing the children, merely taking account of their behaviour under the particular circumstances. As a skilled observer these daily observations are important and can inform your practice and planning.

B. Participatory observation in clinical settings refers to those situations where children attend a clinic or laboratory setting. In general they attend for a specific reason and the observer/assessor has a series of specific questions to answer. It is participatory in that the observer and the child interact. The observer might provide particular play materials and record the child's reactions. The presence of the observer in this situation may affect the way the child behaves and this factor must always be taken into account in analysing observation records at a later date. In a skilled professional the influence can be minimised, the atmosphere relaxed and the child helped feel secure and comfortable. A good account of the use of such observations can be found in Virginia Axline's excellent book *Dibs In Search of Self*.

C. Non-participatory observation in a natural setting is the type of observation you will be carrying out initially. It is through non-participatory observations that you will develop the skill of accurate, objective recording. It involves being in the same room as the children under observation but not interacting with them. You sit back and, as unobtrusively as possible, observe the child or children. You have pen and paper and record what you see as you see it. When observing children it is inappropriate to stare. When you are observing, particularly under these circumstances, you must glance, take in what you see and glance away. Try this out. Prepare to observe, select a child, look directly at her. What do you expect will happen? Her behaviour will become self-conscious and change. It will not be representative of her usual behaviour. Now select another child but this time glance around, only occasionally taking a glance at the selected child. Here you should see a much better sample of usual behaviour.

This type of observation is being increasingly used in the research studies that focus on early childhood care and education. It is considered valuable because the children are more relaxed and one is more likely to get a true picture of the behaviour. Kathy Sylva and her team in the Oxford Preschool Project developed this type of observation to a high level. For their studies they identified a Target Child (TC) and observed this child in particular. As it is important to fade into the background and be unobtrusive it can take a deal of time to settle into the actual recording of material. For students on placement the opportunities should arise once you begin to know the children by name and they have come to accept you as one of the team. Initially it is easier to stand back for short periods to make your record. (It is, of course, essential that you have informed staff of your intentions to do this and received permission.)

D. Non-participatory observation in a clinical setting. The most common way for this to occur is through the use of one-way mirrors. Children may be in a playroom and the end wall is mirrored. They cannot see out but you can see into the room. In this way your presence will not disturb the child. This technique was used by Albert Bandura and his colleagues when studying the way observing aggressive behaviour may affect the play behaviour of young children. In this study young children were given the opportunity, among others, to observe adults behaving in an aggressive way towards a large inflated doll. They were seen to punch, hit, kick and toss it in the air. When the children were observed, using a one-way mirror system, in the playroom with the doll they were found to behave significantly more aggressively and in a manner similar to that observed, than a control group of children who had not seen the adults' behaviour.

There are strengths and weaknesses associated with the different methods of observation. Naturalistic observation is valuable because it allows one to observe children in their natural environment and acquire a more accurate account of their regular behaviour patterns. It is weak because conditions under which observations occur cannot be controlled and may not be the same for all children. Structured observation is useful as it offers a standardised observation situation for all children and a great deal of detailed information can be gathered in a short space of time. Observations, however, may not be typical of children's everyday behaviour and therefore have a limited application.

OBSERVATION RECORDS

There are a wide variety of record types that may be used for recording observations. They vary depending on the aim of the observer. I will refer to the five most commonly used record types: continuous/specimen record, event sampling, time sampling, diary record and checklists.

Continuous/specimen record describes a complete block of behaviour. In training to develop the skill of observing objectively it is a most valuable type of record to keep. It is time consuming but provides a wealth of information. In a study by an American, Laura Berk, this procedure was used to study how sensitive, responsive and verbally stimulating caregivers were when they interacted with preschool children in daycare centres. She recorded everything each caregiver did and said and the amount of time spent away from the children was also included. Analysing this information allowed for improvements in the work style of different staff members and an improvement in the quality of the service provided to the children.

Event sampling is a procedure used when observing a particular behaviour and only records examples of this behaviour. One might want to study the social interaction of a particular child — you will only record her behaviour in situations in which she is in contact with other children or with adults. You may find it necessary to create social situations to get sufficient information and with the record made you can create further opportunities to encourage social interaction.

Time sampling is another approach used in studying child behaviour. Here you choose a period of time during which to record behaviour. You might find, for instance, that just prior to morning snack-time your group become loud and more difficult to manage. A sampling of behaviour occurring during this particular pre-snack time might illuminate factors leading to the increased noise level and allow you to alter certain things to change the situation. In my own research into how nurseries meet the needs of children I used a time sampling/continuous record. I recorded twenty-minute periods of behaviour of individual children. Analysing this material gave a vivid picture of what children do in day nurseries and allowed for interpretation of its value.

Diary records are the type most commonly used in the everyday running of services for children. They may be of little value where the entries are of a brief, subjective nature. However, where staff have been trained in objective observation these records can provide a valuable profile of the ongoing development of children and the effectiveness and quality of the daily programme. In a situation where there appears to be a sudden change in behaviour, for example, a review of the recent diary entries in relation to a particular child may illuminate an emerging pattern and allow for action. In situations where there is team work and staff overlap, these diary records are an important source of continuity for the child. It is important that entries should contain positive as well as negative information. Too often, due to time constraints, one may highlight only what was difficult and omit the small successes and high points of the day!

Checklists: Different authors have developed checklists of expected behaviour for children of different ages and abilities. Examples can be found in many text-books. The intention is that staff are provided with a graded list of behaviours and tick, as a result of observation, those behaviours that a particular child is capable of. There is a danger that too much reliance on the checklist may lead to the 'non-observation' of other, equally important behaviour! Caution is necessary. One good checklist or record that has been developed for working with young children in a group setting is the Keele Preschool Assessment Guide(KPAG). Below is a sample from that guide.

DEVELOPING THE SKILL OF OBSERVATION

Practice and honesty are the two basic requirements to developing the skill of observation. Without practice we may believe we have the skill but in fact are relying on interpretation and opinion rather than objective detail. In practice you should set yourself tasks, test yourself and, as far as possible, honestly evaluate your records. It is only you who can really know how accurately you are recording what you see.

SOCIALISATION*

S1. Self Help
1. Cares for self at toilet and washes hands satisfactorily.
2. Uses knife, fork and spoon.
3. Manages simple fastenings.
4. Manages zips.
5. Dresses self completely.

S2. Play Patterns
1. Plays in parallel with others and will take turns.
2. Understands concept of sharing; plays associatively.
3. Plays co-operatively with companions.
4. Plays simple games with rules.
5. Understands winning and losing.

*From: KPAG Record Form.

Cultivate the roving eye: when walking or travelling look around more closely. Note things and try to describe them: the day is grey, but what else can you say about it? There are a lot of advertising hoardings on the way home: how many, what type?

Cultivate the roving mind: as well as becoming more observant try to assess the meaning of what you observe. Why are there no advertising hoardings here but lots there? Why is it that playgrounds are situated where they are . . . and so on. The development of a questioning mind is helpful in overcoming our tendency to accept things on face value in an unquestioning way.

USE OF THE OBSERVATION MATERIAL — CONFIDENTIALITY

In any situation relating to closely observed material there is the question of who should see the records. In a training situation the record may only be seen by the observer and a tutor. Careful maintenance of confidentiality is important here and we recommend that the name of the children observed not be included on the record.

In the work situation any service providing for children and maintaining records must develop a policy on what information is kept on file and on what material is made available to whom:

• All the staff working with children or just the manager and key worker?

- Other professionals who might have contact with the service — public health nurses, social workers and so on.

- Professionals (such as teachers) working in other agencies or institutions the child may attend.

- Students who may be on placement with the children.

- Parents of the children.

There would be general agreement that all staff working with the children should have access to files. This is important because background information is valuable in seeking explanations for particular behaviour. Also shared access allows for continuity in the sharing of the care of the children. In certain circumstances it is agreed that other professionals should have access. It may be to a briefer file rather than one filled with everyday detail or it might be the complete record. The decision on this should be a central policy of which all staff, and parents are aware.

Many centres restrict access to records in the case of students. The staff are often willing to answer general questions about background but will not make files available. For any student on placement it is important to clarify the policy of the placement and abide by this policy.

Whether parents have access to records is something that can generate a lot of debate and discussion. Historically parents have tended to be excluded from access to this kind of material but over recent years there has been a move towards greater openness. There is no requirement on staff to provide access to records in preschool services and some staff may be concerned that if parents have access the quality of the reports might alter or parents might react angrily where records contained details of both appropriate and inappropriate behaviour. However, Jenny Laishley disagrees that this is a realistic concern. In her book *Working with Young Children* she identifies six reasons why records should be on open access to parents.

The general view is that parents should have access to the records and that the advantages of this far outweigh the disadvantages. Even in situations where children are cared for in small groups, such as childminding or family daycare, brief records with basic information and a record of progress should be maintained.

1. As parents have a long-term responsibility for the well-being of their children they have a right to see the records/opinions of the adults who temporarily share the responsibility of caring for their children.
2. Most parents would be interested in the records as they are interested in the progress of their children. The material may also be helpful to them.
3. Where factual errors have occurred the parent can correct this.
4. When records are on open access to parents it allows for the exchange and sharing of information. People can learn from each other.
5. If records are closed, unsupported opinions and flawed interpretations may be allowed to go unquestioned.
6. Where records are on closed access it creates a suspicion that something uncomplimentary has been written.

The Data Protection Act 1988 details the responsibility of staff with respect to records and the law requires, for example, that personal information on computer must be available to the individuals concerned. Further information can be had from the Data Protection Commissioner, Block 4, Irish Life Centre, Talbot Street, Dublin 1.

SUMMARY

Observation is a skill that is essential in working successfully with young children. By developing the skill of objective observation we can override our very human tendency to make quick judgments and interpretations which may reflect personal bias rather than actual fact.

To develop the skill of objective observation, the importance of practice cannot be overstressed. How to prepare for an observation and when to use a particular record sheet in work with young children must be carefully planned. For practice it is recommended that the Target Child (TC) technique be used in at least some of your observations.

Observation is valuable as it allows one to see beyond the immediate activity or situation. It further allows one to draw on theoretical knowledge to explain particular behaviour. Different settings in which observations can occur are outlined.

Important issues for consideration include record keeping and the important subject of access and confidentiality.

EXERCISES

1. What is the difference between *objective* and *subjective* observation? Which is more natural to the human?

2. With a partner, discuss and write down some of the reasons for developing the skill of objective observation.

3. What is a Target Child (TC)?

4. List the four sections one would find on a TC record sheet. Select one and give more details.

5. List the five different record types outlined in the chapter. Select two and identify the differences.

6. Observe one of the following: a playgroup, a playhouse, a nursery group or a playground. Carefully record all that you notice.

7. Observe a child at: waterplay, sandplay, home corner, art or snack-time. Record *only* the behaviour observed. Read your record closely and discuss your findings with a partner.

8. Observe and record the interaction between a mother/carer and infant at bath-time, feeding-time, changing-time or bedtime. Write a short discussion on what you have recorded.

9. Observe and record two young children in conversation. Identify the setting and comment on your record.

10. Carry out a five minute, continuous structured observation on a child of your choice. On completion of the record write a brief discussion on what you observed. Try to ensure that you only record what you actually *see*.

chapter 4
child development

Understanding the way children develop is a basic prerequisite to working effectively with them. Those of us who choose to work with children are, generally speaking, interested in children. Developmental psychology is that branch of psychology interested in understanding human behaviour and how it develops. Here we are interested, specifically, in the study of child development. Psychologists *describe* behaviour — what exactly a young child does when a stranger approaches, for instance. They *measure* behaviour, in this way allowing for comparison between children in different settings and of different ages and finally they attempt to *explain* behaviour.

This pattern of *describe*, *measure* and *explain* is not exclusive to the psychologist and indeed is a valuable guide to understanding behaviour for anyone working with children. Despite the rather obvious nature of the pattern it is not always easy to describe behaviour. With young children, however, the task is perhaps easiest as much of their development is visible through their actions. Working with young children therefore affords an excellent opportunity to observe closely and, as far as possible, objectively. This observation then yields description, measurement and, at least potentially, explanation.

So what have psychologists discovered about child development? In the first place it has become clear that common patterns of development exist. For instance, Stranger Anxiety — where a young child expresses unease in the presence of a stranger by crying — is a worldwide phenomenon in children between the ages of eight to twelve months. It has been found that the intensity varies from child to child but the behaviour is common. Similarly, with walking alone — this has been found to occur, universally, at around thirteen months. These ages must be

considered with some caution, however. For instance, my eldest daughter walked alone at eleven months: my second daughter, however, did not walk until she was twenty-two months old! She was mobile much earlier as she had refined a bottom shuffling routine which left her hands free to explore the world. She was not hampered by her late walking and so it caused no great concern. Recognising 'normal' ages for the achievement of milestones is valuable but taking account of the individual child is also important. Where differences are found between individual children or a group of children, psychologists are interested in understanding why. What factors account for differences among children? For example, does the health of the mother during pregnancy affect the unborn child's potential? What are young, newborn infants able to do? Can they see, hear, can they think? Can you speed up development? Is it advisable to try and speed up development? Do babies need to be with their natural mothers or do other caring arrangements work as effectively? Does long-term daycare affect the older child? These and many other questions are of interest to those studying child development.

THE VALUE OF STUDYING CHILD DEVELOPMENT

Why should we be interested in finding out so much about children? There are three reasons at least:

1. If we know what to expect at different ages we are less inclined to worry about the individual differences that can arise. We will not get upset if a three-year-old has a temper tantrum or if a four-year-old stutters over words in an effort to make an important point.

2. If we know what to expect we can provide appropriate materials and activity opportunities. Knowing what to expect allows us look out for 'readiness'. There is little point in expecting a two-year-old to read a sentence. However, even at this early age children are literate — they will recognise signs such as a particular breakfast cereal or a letter from their name. It is therefore valuable to extend the literate experiences they have.

3. By being sensitive to what is developmentally appropriate we can spot delays in development and act as necessary.

In coming to understand children's development and what to expect at different stages we must also take account of personal factors. Our own views about children, our values and attitudes may influence the way we answer questions asked by them.

NATURE OR NURTURE OR BOTH?

Our views, for example, on the fundamental nature of childhood can affect the way we interpret their behaviours. Do we believe that children are born the way they are, or do they become the way they are? How much influence does inheritance have and how much does experience influence development?

There has been considerable controversy over the relative contribution of **environmental** factors, such as stability of the family, amount of education, wealth, and **biological** factors, such as genes, to the development and change in behaviour. This debate is known as the Nature (Biology) versus Nurture (Environment) debate and will be referred to on occasion throughout the book. Although there may be different levels of interaction between these factors it is now believed that most development owes something to both nature and nurture. No area of development can be considered as exclusively biologically determined or exclusively environmentally controlled. For instance, the potential for development of the young orphans in the Romanian orphanages, seen on our TV screens in 1990, was severely curtailed by the deficiencies in their environment. Without adequate environmental stimulation to support the children they could not achieve their developmental milestones at the appropriate age and were found to be seriously delayed in their motor, linguistic, social and intellectual development. There were some fixed characteristics determined by their genetic inheritance such as their sex, their hair and eye colour but beyond these factors biological potential depends on environmental support.

ARE CHILDREN ACTIVE OR PASSIVE IN THEIR DEVELOPMENT?

Do you consider children to be active agents in their own development and learning or do you see them as passive? Do children learn or are they taught? These questions are basic to how we treat children. In our ordinary contact with children, we may not give it a second thought, but in the context of working with children, particularly through the formative early years, it is important to understand our own views on children and what influences their behaviour. Research that has originated from the work of Jean Piaget including that by Jerome Bruner, Margaret Donaldson and others suggests that children are indeed active in their learning and not the passive receptors waiting for information and knowledge as was believed in years past. Accepting that children are actively involved in their own development — and in some measure in control of it — we, as adults, must admit to limited control over them and their learning. We cannot force them to learn until they are developmentally ready. By understanding the process of development we can provide experiences and opportunities that will interest and challenge children at an appropriate level. The National Association for the Education of Young Children, an American organisation concerned with high quality early provision for young children, has published a booklet discussing developmentally appropriate practice. For instance, in relation to infants they give the following examples:

- **Appropriate Practice (AP):** that children have their own cots, bedding, feeding utensils, nappies, soothers and any special comfort object. The infant's name should be used to label every personal item.

- **Inappropriate Practice (IP):** that children share sleeping quarters in shifts, or do not have their own supplies.

- **AP:** A variety of music is provided for enjoyment in listening/body movement/singing.

- **IP:** Music is used to distract or lull infants to sleep. Children hear only children's songs.

- **AP:** Books are heavy cardboard with rounded edges. They have bright pictures of familiar objects.

- **IP:** Books are not available, or are made of paper that tears easily. Books do not contain objects familiar or interesting to infants. Faded colours or intricate drawings are used.

We will return again to the subject of appropriate practice in the final sections of the book but the above gives an idea of what I am talking about.

THE COMPETENT CHILD

The child, from the earliest moments of her life, is trying to make sense of her world and to exercise some self-directed control over it. Even very young babies show a preference for complexity and contrast in their environment and this will be discussed later under the heading of perception.

Thus we must endeavour to consider the children with whom we work — no matter how young — as competent human beings and not the desperately vulnerable creatures sometimes portrayed. When studying children and their development it is necessary to look at different aspects of development separately. This helps focus attention on a particular area to notice the shifts from one stage to the next. All areas of development, however, interact and we must never lose sight of the whole child. For instance, while studying the pattern of physical development you will notice how important an area it is to the social development of the child. A child's confidence and self-esteem is often strengthened by their control in the area of physical skills.

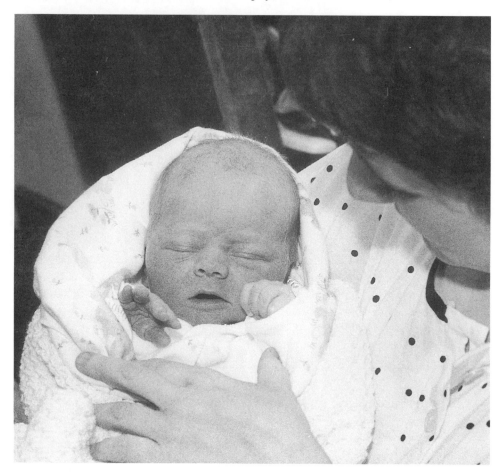

In studies of children we view the child in terms of body and mind and isolate the various aspects of development — physical, social, language, intellectual and emotional — for special attention. In so doing we simplify the task of describing and understanding development but must be careful not to render the child too simplistic a being; their complexity reflects the intricate interactions of the various aspects of development and their interdependence on each other. Every individual is more than the sum of their parts: this essence is hard to define but can be considered as the spirit of the person. This essence of the child, or spirit of the child, is an important element to consider. It refers to the child's developing awareness of self and others, the emergence of a sense of wonder at the world and the importance of the imagination. It is often an important guide to the complex life of the child. The development of the spirit within us is the development of the humanity we share with others. It is our nature as humans. What a child experiences influences this growth. To experience love, acceptance and welcome facilitates the development of humanity. To experience rejection, ignoring and ridicule is to retard this development.

In working with children we must try to develop prosocial and humane characteristics. Even with children as young as two years we can facilitate the development of empathy, of being able to imagine the happiness or sadness of another. This acknowledgment of nature can extend to plants and animals — a child's wonder at the simple things like the sprouting of a hyacinth bulb, or the falling snow or a rainbow should be cultivated and treasured. It is this wonder and reverence which facilitates the development of a caring, co-operative adult. A simple 'thanks' after a meal or a treat means more to a child than a lengthy, but abstract or habitual, grace before meals: it is a more visible and concrete occasion for thanks. Rather than repeat a learned-by-heart thanks in words that are unfamiliar it is more meaningful to draw children's attention to a lovely moment and allow children a little time to dwell on it. No doubt many of us remember the errors in our own prayers reflecting our lack of understanding of the words we used. Certainly let us celebrate events like Christmas, Easter and Saints' days and include, where appropriate, the celebrations of other cultures and let us nurture the spirit of the child within. But we must be cautious: too early a presentation of concepts of religion may be confusing and meaningless as these are difficult concepts for children to grasp. Young children do not have the power of understanding that children over seven years of age have and so cannot appreciate the significance of religious concepts. The manner in which this important area is introduced is crucial and if it is too directive or authoritarian it may, in the long run, inhibit the development and growth of the child's own personal spirituality.

BEGINNINGS: THE PRENATAL PERIOD

The life of each individual begins when the sperm from the father penetrates the egg (ovum) from the mother. This penetration sets in motion a process of cell division until thousands of cells have been produced. Gradually over time the cells take on specific functions — some as part of the nervous system, others as part of the muscle, skeletal or circulatory system.

The fertilised egg becomes like a ball of cells and gradually takes shape into the foetus. After approximately nine months the foetus is ready for birth. All cells in the human body contain forty-six chromosomes, twenty-three from the father and twenty-three from the mother. When the sperm penetrates the wall of the ovum it releases its twenty-three chromosomes. At the same time the nucleus (central core) of the ovum breaks up to release its twenty-three chromosomes. These two groups pair into twenty-three pairs (forty-six in total) and each cell subsequently formed contains this new combination of chromosomes yielding a new and unique individual. All the child's biological heritage, the blueprint for development, is contained in these forty-six chromosomes. Each chromosome is subdivided into genes — some 20,000 per chromosome. The gene is the basic unit of inheritance and is made up of a substance called Deoxyribonucleic Acid or DNA.

Most of the cells making up the human are called body cells and contain twenty-three pairs of chromosomes. However, the new individual is created by the union of two special cells — the sperm and the ovum — and they are referred to as germ cells or gametes. They are unique in that they contain only twenty-three single chromosomes, half as many as a regular cell. When the sperm and the ovum unite at fertilisation to form the beginning of the new individual, the cell that results — called the zygote — will have forty-six chromosomes. Using microscopic techniques the pairs of chromosomes can be distinguished from one another. Twenty-two pairs are called autosomes and they are numbered by geneticists from longest to shortest 1–22. The twenty-third pair of chromosomes is known as the sex chromosome. In females the pair is denoted by XX and in the male by XY. The single X is a relatively large chromosome; the Y on the other hand, is short and carries relatively little genetic material. In gamete formation in males the X and Y separate into the separate sperm cells while all the female gametes (ova) contain an X chromosome. The sex of a new individual is determined by whether an X-bearing or a Y-bearing sperm fertilises the egg. This is illustrated in the diagram below.

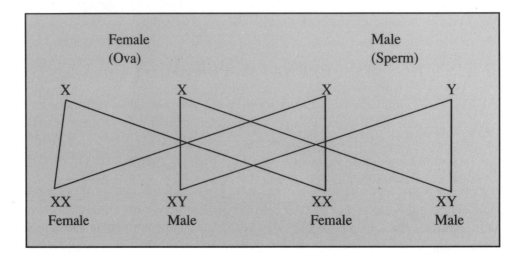

The order of prenatal development is genetically programmed and the environment in which the foetus develops is the very stable environment of the womb. Except in cases of extreme deprivation the womb of one woman is very similar to that of another. The stability of the environment allows us to accurately determine the level of development of the baby at the various stages throughout the prenatal period. This process of prenatal development is commonly divided into three separate periods: the period of the *zygote,* the period of the *embryo* and the period of the *foetus.*

The period of the zygote lasts for two weeks, from the fertilisation until the cell bundle attaches to the lining of the uterus. Occasionally during this period the first two cells produced after fertilisation separate and give rise to two individuals. These will be *identical* or *monozygotic(MZ)* (from one zygote) twins and represent the only occasion where two individuals have the same genetic make-up. This fact has had important implications for those studies concerning the relative effects of nature versus nurture because, it has been argued, any differences between identical twins can only be explained in terms of environmental factors. *Fraternal* or *dizygotic(DZ)* (from two zygotes) twins arise where the mother has released two eggs, or ova, both of which are fertilised. Fraternal twins are no more alike than any ordinary siblings. By the end of this period the zygote has begun to grow and differentiate.

The period of the embryo: From implantation to about eight weeks the organism is called the embryo. There is rapid growth during the embryonic period and by four weeks the embryo is just visible to the naked eye. At five weeks it is approximately five mm in length and the spine is beginning to form. By six weeks there is clear formation of the head, chest and small depressions where the eyes and ears will be situated. Further rapid development occurs so that by the eighth week all the major internal organs are formed, although still at a very rudimentary stage and the face is beginning to assume recognisable characteristics. The head enlarges and by the end of the second month some movement is possible. This movement is too light to be felt by the mother. Now, although only 2.2 cm in length, everything that will be found in the newborn infant is present.

The period of the foetus: This is the longest phase of development and is a period of growth and 'finishing off'. The organism is now called the foetus and, as most of the vital parts have been formed, is less vulnerable to the influences of factors such as drugs and disease. The rate of body growth is very rapid during this period particularly in the earlier stages. From eight to twelve weeks there is development and refinement and the foetus becomes more recognisable as a small human being. Prenatal development is divided into three trimesters or periods of three months and the twelfth week represents the end of the first trimester.

WHAT ARE THE CAPACITIES OF THE FOETUS?

By the middle of the second trimester the movement of the foetus can be felt by the mother. The baby is now clearly distinguishable and the limbs and joints are properly formed. The foetus, if 'born', would not be viable as the lungs, although structurally complete, are still immature. The remainder of the pregnancy is designed to allow the foetus to grow to a size and with organs sufficiently developed to allow for survival. The end of the second trimester is significant for psychologists as it marks the earliest stage of learning in the human baby.

AN IMPORTANT STUDY INTO FETAL LEARNING

In the 1940s a researcher called Spelt carried out a seminal piece of work. Taking mothers in their sixth month he recorded the level of activity of the foetus in the womb to obtain a benchmark or baseline of fetal activity. He then created a loud noise in the area close to the foetus and recorded the activity level and, as expected, the level rose as the foetus gave a 'startle' response to the loud noise. Following this, Spelt applied a gentle vibrator over the stomach of the women and recorded the activity level of the foetus. Under this condition the foetus presented a lower activity level than the baseline. Having secured this information he then created a situation in which he aimed to 'teach' the foetus to increase activity level to the vibrator. If this could be shown to happen, Spelt argued, you could consider that the foetus was capable of learning in the womb. This is precisely what did happen.

By following the vibrator with a five second pause and then a loud noise he found that the foetus yielded an increased activity level to the vibrator once there was a consistent link with the loud noise. It was as if the foetus learned that the application of the vibrator signalled the arrival of the loud sound. This study is important because it suggests that the environment of the child is influential before birth and that the foetus is capable of rudimentary, simple learning.

Over the remaining weeks the foetus is getting ready for birth. By thirty-two weeks the foetus is fully formed and has a 95% chance of survival if born in optimum circumstances. At forty weeks the foetus is ready for delivery and birth is imminent.

PRENATAL INFLUENCES ON DEVELOPMENT

A discussion of factors affecting prenatal development is important as it useful for those working with children to understand the influence of prenatal experiences on the development and behaviour of the individual. Most babies born are healthy and well. Some, however, are less healthy and may suffer from specific, identifiable disorders which affect their later development. A wide variety of factors, from fertilisation through the prenatal period can affect the well-being of the developing organism and these will be discussed in greater detail below.

BIOLOGICAL FACTORS AFFECTING PRENATAL DEVELOPMENT

At the point of fertilisation there is some potential for damage to the zygote and abnormal transfer of genetic material may occur. We have mentioned that a normal sperm and ovum contain twenty-three chromosomes each. Most chromosomal defects occur as a result of imperfect development of the gametes where part of a chromosome may break off or where a pair of chromosomes has failed to separate properly at crossover. Since chromosomal error involves far more of the genetic material Deoxyribonucleic Acid (DNA) than problems associated with a single gene they usually produce disorders that display a wide variety of physical as well as mental symptoms with depressed intellectual functioning being one common outcome. The most common chromosomal abnormality is Down's Syndrome where an extra chromosome is transferred at fertilisation so that the developing organism contains forty-seven rather than forty-six chromosomes. Down's Syndrome is due to one of several different types of chromosomal error. In over 90% of cases it results from the failure of the twenty-first chromosomal pair to separate and is sometimes referred to as Trisomy 21 (containing three 21 chromosomes). The diagram below outlines this transfer error:

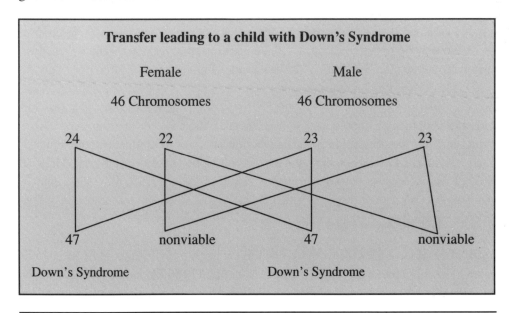

Transfer leading to a child with Down's Syndrome

Female   Male

46 Chromosomes   46 Chromosomes

24   22   23   23

47   nonviable   47   nonviable

Down's Syndrome   Down's Syndrome

In the remainder of cases it can occur where a piece of broken 21 chromosome joins the twenty-first pair at fertilisation. Children born with Down's Syndrome show a number of clear characteristics such as a stocky build, flattened face, almond shaped eyes and an unusual crease running across the palm of the hand. Such children may also exhibit heart defects and/or breathing and feeding difficulties. Children with Down's Syndrome have learning difficulties but some may show greater abilities than others and in a small percentage of cases may, for example, learn to read. Many children with Down's Syndrome are friendly, easygoing and placid in disposition. They enjoy attention and, with a stimulating early environment, the quality of their development can be improved. There is an increased effort in Ireland, as elsewhere, to develop high quality early educational supports for such children and, where possible to integrate them into the services available for all children.

There are a wide variety of other, rarer cases of chromosomal abnormalities and some of these are associated with transfer of the sex chromosomes. One such disorder is known as Turner's Syndrome where, at fertilisation, only one X chromosome is transferred. The individual born with this pattern of chromosomes appears as a female but there is impairment of ovary development and the development of secondary sexual characteristics rendering most infertile. Early identification and hormonal treatment may lessen the effect of the syndrome on individual girls.

GENES: DOMINANT AND RECESSIVE

Other defects may arise as a result of a gene defect rather than a chromosomal defect. As mentioned earlier each chromosome is made up of many thousands of genes and in some cases a problem may arise. Genes can be either *dominant* or *recessive*. Recessive genes can only be effective if they are linked with another recessive gene when chromosomes pair up after fertilisation. Otherwise the dominant gene is effective. Many of our characteristics are controlled by more complex patterns of gene combination: they are polygenic. Hair colour, however, results from a single gene influence. The gene for dark hair is dominant (represented by the letter H), the gene for fair hair is recessive (represented by the letter h). Individuals who inherit a pair of dominant genes HH and those who inherit a gene pair Hh both have dark hair. The *genotype* is different (HH and Hh) but the *phenotype*, the physical manifestation of the gene pattern, is the same — dark hair. Fair hair can only emerge when the individual inherits the combination of two recessive genes (hh).

Many diseases have been identified as resulting from the combination of two recessive genes. The most frequently cited example is called Phenylketonuria (PKU). Infants with PKU carry two recessive genes, labelled pp, which results in the lack of an enzyme (phenylalanine hydroxylase) that converts a potentially harmful amino acid contained in protein into a harmless by-product. In the absence of this enzyme the toxic phenylalanine accumulates in the infant and damages the central nervous system. Untreated, the child will become mentally retarded.

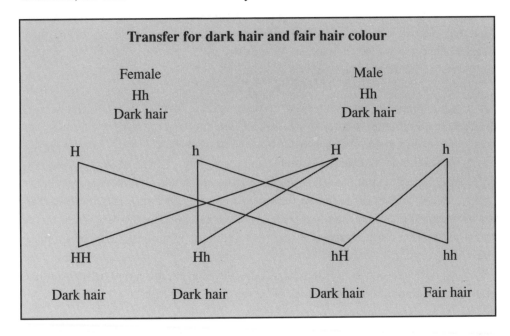

Transfer for dark hair and fair hair colour

In Ireland all newborns are tested for PKU shortly after birth. If it is diagnosed the baby can be placed on a special diet which is low in phenylalanine and the damaging effects are avoided. This diet is generally adhered to long term to avoid any build up of the toxic material.

ENVIRONMENTAL FACTORS AFFECTING PRENATAL DEVELOPMENT

Environmental agents that cause damage during the prenatal period are called *teratogens*. The most well-known teratogen is maternal Rubella (German Measles). If contracted by the mother during the first trimester it leads to varying degrees of physical defects in the newborn. In Ireland all children can now receive a free Rubella vaccine to counteract the likelihood of contracting the disease and so reduce the incidence of Rubella in general. Another well-documented teratogen is the tranquilliser Thalidomide. During the 1960s this was freely available but, when taken by a certain group of pregnant women, led to gross deformities in the limbs of the infants born. The time at which teratogens are most likely to affect the foetus detrimentally varies, but there are critical periods where the effect can be most damaging. These periods are associated with the stages of most rapid development or differentiation in the foetus.

Other teratogens include radiation and environmental pollution which can cause changes in the structure of the genes and may lead to serious damage to the foetus. Maternal age can also have an effect. Older mothers and teenage mothers are more likely to experience complications but if healthy and in good care the risk to mother and baby can be minimised.

The emotional state of the mother, her nutrition and her level of nicotine, alcohol and drug intake all influence the sensitive foetus. These factors can have long-term effects on the infant. For instance babies born to stressed mothers are more likely to have a low birth weight, be hyperactive, irritable and show poor patterns of sleeping and eating. These factors within the infant can then affect the quality of interaction with the mother following the birth and so their effect can be quite far-reaching. Maternal disease caused by viral infections also affects the foetus. A relatively new illness that is spreading among certain groups of mothers and their infants is Acquired Immune Deficiency Syndrome (AIDS) associated with the HIV virus. Like other viral infections AIDS can be transmitted across the placental barrier to the foetus from the mother and the infant is at serious risk of contracting the disease.

BIRTH

Following the nine month gestation period the baby is ready for delivery. This begins with contractions which lead, finally, to birth. This period is called labour and divided into three stages.

1. Dilation and effacement of the cervix: This is the longest stage of labour lasting up to twelve hours with a first baby. The contractions cause the cervix to thin and widen so that the baby can enter the birth canal. The contractions gradually become more intense.

2. Expulsion of the foetus: This is a much shorter stage as the baby moves down the birth canal and is finally born. It is the mother's pushing, combined with further contractions of the uterus, that force the baby down and out.

3. Expulsion of the placenta: In this final stage the placenta detaches from the uterine wall and a few contractions and pushes by the mother cause it to be expelled from the birth canal.

Despite the fact that birth is a traumatic experience for the infant and mother alike, most births take place normally and result in healthy newborn infants who adapt quickly to their new environment. There are, however, some complications that can occur and may affect later development. The ease or difficulty with which a delivery occurs and the rapidity with which the newborn begins to breathe can affect the infant's well-being. There are a number of difficulties that can arise at birth but the two major ones involve damage to the blood vessels of the brain; *haemorrhaging* caused by strong pressure on the head of the foetus and *failure to begin to breathe* on separation from the mother's oxygen source. Both these factors affect the supply of oxygen to the nerve cells of the brain and in extreme cases can lead to damaged nerve cells and subsequent physical and psychological defects. This lack of oxygen or the delay in oxygen reaching the brain is called *Anoxia*. The nerve cells, or neurons, in the Central Nervous System (CNS) require oxygen: if deprived some cells will die and cannot be replaced. If too many of the cells die the infant will suffer serious brain damage. With mild anoxia the differences in behaviour between normal children and mildly anoxic children diminish with age and there is no firm evidence of permanent or serious intellectual damage.

PREMATURITY

Premature children are those born early: slightly premature refers to birth at thirty-four to thirty-eight weeks; intermediate term at thirty to thirty-three weeks and extreme prematurity where a child is born at less than twenty-six weeks. Premature babies are vulnerable to environmental effects for some years after birth. In supportive, nurturing and loving homes they show little long-term damage but premature babies born to families in impoverished conditions or to mothers who had poor prenatal care are more likely than full-term babies to suffer difficulties both physical and psychological.

POSTMATURITY

Delayed birth, postmaturity, may also constitute a threat to the newborn due to factors related to difficult delivery, inadequate prenatal nutrition in the later stages of pregnancy and the danger from a build-up of noxious material. They, like premature babies, require expert care and attention.

SUMMARY

This chapter considered the way in which child development is studied and identifies some of the reasons for the interest in the area.

A major area of interest to researchers and those of us working directly with children relates to how much of our behaviour is inherited and how much is acquired, or learned. This is known as the Nature/Nurture debate and is outlined.

From careful observation of children we now know that they are quite competent and that all of their senses are working by the time they are born, although not to the refined level of older children and adults. Our knowledge of child development should influence the way we work with children and help us ensure that we provide developmentally appropriate experiences for children.

The process of prenatal development is an ordered one. There are dangers to the developing foetus and these include factors related to genetic transfer and to environmental factors, teratogens. The birth process is also an ordered procedure and there are a small number of difficulties that can arise and these include prematurity and anoxia.

EXERCISES

1. Write down some of the reasons why it is important to study the development of children.

2. What is meant by the Nature/Nurture debate? What other words could you use in place of Nature and Nurture?

3. Do children learn in an active or a passive way? How might this knowledge affect your practice with young children?

4. What is meant by the term 'developmentally appropriate'? Give an example of developmentally appropriate and inappropriate practice for:

   • a six-month-old

   • a two-year-old

   • a four-year-old.

5. What do the initials DNA mean?

6. What is the difference between a gene and a chromosome? What is a dominant gene?

7. What is meant by:

   • a zygote

   • a gamcte

   • an autosome

   • dizygotic

8. Briefly describe the experiment carried out by Spelt. Why is it so important?
9. Select two factors that can influence the development of the foetus and describe the possible effects.

10. What are the primary risks to the baby at birth?

chapter 5
physical and perceptual development

The womb is a well-protected environment. After birth the newborn now experiences hunger, cold, heat, pain and is forced to react in order to overcome the discomfort and adapt to this new environment. Typically the newborn cries when hungry or uncomfortable and later, vocalises with coos and gurgles when content.

THE NEWBORN OR NEONATE

The belief that 'the world of the baby is a blooming, buzzing confusion', proposed by William James in the 1890s, owes much to the assumption that the infant is a passive and helpless creature. Recent research (Robert Fantz, Tom Bower) suggests, however, that the infant's world is a lot less confusing than presumed. The organisation of newborn behaviour is quite different from that of older babies, children and adults but it is not random or a confusion and the baby appears to be an active agent in the communications and interactions that occur.

The newborn period covers the first five to seven days after birth. The baby is establishing a balance with the surrounding environment. We saw in the last chapter that the foetus in the womb can hear by the sixth month of development. We know that from the moment of birth, unlike other young, e.g. puppies, the human infant can see, hear, smell and taste and is also sensitive to pain, touch and a change in position. To take taste: from the first hours after birth babies show a strong preference for sweet tastes. They will suck faster and harder to get the taste of sugar water than to get plain water and they seem disappointed when sugar water is followed by plain water. This disappointment is evident from their tendency to suck less vigorously for plain water *after* tasting the sugar water than if they have only tasted plain water. This sweet taste is a characteristic that persists into adulthood.

The newborn baby is also equipped with a wide range of reflexive behaviours. Reflexes are the newborn's organised patterns of behaviour. Some of the more common ones are outlined below.

SOME NEONATAL REFLEXES

Reflex	Stimulation	Significance
Rooting reflex	Tickle corner of the mouth	Assists baby in finding the nipple.
Sucking reflex	Place index finger 3 cm into mouth.	Permits feeding. Weak in depressed infants.
Moro reflex Back arches, arms and legs extend and move back towards the midline in a 'hug'.	Support body horizontally, allow head 'drop' a few cm.	A weak Moro reflex indicates disturbance of the Central Nervous System.
Knee jerk reflex	Tap on tendon just below the knee.	Absent in depressed infants or in cases of muscular disease.
Babinski reflex	Stroke sole of infant's foot, from toes to heel.	Absent in infants with defects of lower spine.

One of the most interesting is the Moro Reflex. Infants show this reaction to a sudden change in head position. The infant throws the arms out to the side, extends her fingers and then brings her arms and hands back to the midline — as if hugging someone. This reflex has a developmental significance. It is present up to three to four months but is difficult to elicit after six months. This is because the central nervous system is taking over control of behaviour from the more primitive lower and midbrain centres. If the Moro Reflex is found in older babies it would be worrying as it would suggest that the central nervous system is not taking over control as expected. The upper cortical region is very immature at birth and will not be fully mature until puberty, although 90% of brain growth is achieved by the time a child is six.

Reflexes regulate a lot of the behaviours seen in young infants but as the child develops and as the brain begins to mature these reflexes give way to voluntary behaviour. This transformation from newborn reflexes to cortically controlled behaviour is perfectly normal. Babies are born with immature brains because if their heads were any bigger there would be an increased likelihood of damage at birth. Nature has left higher brain growth to the postnatal period of infancy and childhood.

Babies can see — although not as efficiently as older children and adults. They can track a moving object and will follow a moving object with their eyes. They are also interested in staring at novel or complex patterns and seem particularly to like staring at the human face. The newborn establishes a sleep-wake pattern over the early months. They are able to cry and this crying acts as a means of communicating with the caregivers, and elicits, in general, a fairly immediate reaction. There is some dispute about how quickly one should respond to a baby crying. It is not really possible to spoil a baby in the first months of life. Babies who cry a great deal require parents and carers to work hard at calming them. Crying has the power to elicit a strong and immediate response in most adults. For some adults a child crying at all, however, can be a source of unreasonable irritation. This may affect the quality and success of the interaction between the child and adult and may lead to a more distressing situation. If parents or carers are not successful at calming their child they may feel inadequate and their attitude to the child may become hostile. The alert, quiet baby seems likely to have a smoother relationship with the parents than the baby who is irritable and inclined to cry. A number of different cries have been identified: the basic cry, the cry of anger, the cry of pain and the cry for attention. When a baby is crying and needs to be soothed she should be picked up, held closely, lifted to the shoulder and rocked. Clearly if hungry or uncomfortable, this should be seen to also. The causes of crying are complex and the caregiver must take account of all the factors when crying occurs. No one would suggest that you let a young baby cry out a cry. In the early months the cry should be responded to quickly and calmly. As they get older it is possible to discourage crying and encourage alternative forms of communication.

INFANCY

There is a sequential nature to motor development as can be seen from the Table below.

Motor development in infancy

Motor Skill	Average age achieved
Holds head erect and steady when held upright	7 weeks
When prone, lifts self by arms	2 months
Rolls from side to back	2 months
Rolls from back to side	4.5 months
Grasps cube	4 months
Sits alone	7 months
Pulls to stand up	8 months
Uses Pincer grasp	9 months
Plays 'peek-a-boo'	10 months
Stands alone	11 months
Walks alone	12 months

The quality of motor development has a profound effect on other aspects of development. Both *maturation* (nature) and *experience* (nurture) affect motor development. While the blueprint for the pattern of motor development is laid down in the genetic code of each individual the experiences of the infant are important to overall motor control. The plight of the young children raised in Romanian institutions illustrates this point well. Confined, as many were, to lying in cribs for long periods they showed severe retardation in the emergence of their gross motor skills such as sitting, creeping and walking. Research on babies born blind, quoted by Berk in her book *Child Development* also emphasises the importance of experience to the development of motor skills. Without the advantage of sight as an early means for locating and responding to people and objects, blind babies tend to be passive and not inclined to evoke responses from caregivers to the same degree as their sighted peers. As a result — besides their visual deprivation — many blind babies are also deprived of the touch and sound stimulation that come from being picked up, talked to and played with frequently.

During the first year of life the baby develops from the immobile state of the early months to a restless, eager, mobile child at around a year. By twelve months some babies are walking, some standing supported and others are crawling or scooting about. Once walking, children refine the skill so that they walk with greater control, can carry objects from place to place and can run. From the age of two onwards children become very adventurous — climbing stairs and chairs, dancing, balancing, jumping, kicking, hopping and skipping. These motor skills are called gross motor skills and refer to postural development and the control of large movements. Refining gross motor skills is very enjoyable for children. One just has to watch them in an open space or with garden and playground equipment where they push, pull, swing, slide, cycle and run around. The refinement of fine motor skills — hand/eye co-ordination, reaching, grasping and manipulation — comes more slowly. By six months the baby will reach out to grasp an object. They grasp a rattle or block using the Palmer grasp — this is a whole hand grasp — rather than the more effective Pincer grasp, using the thumb and forefinger as an adult would when picking up a small object.

Objects are frequently put to the mouth at this stage encouraging the development of hand/eye control. The palmer grasp gives way to the pincer grasp at around a year. At this stage the child can hold two blocks and bang them together. Building with blocks emerges at around eighteen months where a tower of three to four blocks may be built. At this stage also the child holds a crayon or thick pencil, can scribble and begins to thread spools and beads. Fine motor skills develop rapidly over the next two to three years. By two-and-a-half years the child can pick up very small objects with thumb and forefinger and can copy a vertical line. There is a developing interest in art and other creative activities requiring fine motor control such as cutting, pasting, building, moulding and printing.

PERCEPTUAL DEVELOPMENT

Another less obvious, but nonetheless important aspect of development is the refinement of the senses or perceptual development. Perception refers to the detection, organisation and interpretation of information from the environment. As you can imagine perception is an important prerequisite to other aspects of development such as thinking and problem-solving. All the knowledge the infant acquires about the world comes through the senses. We have six senses — sight, hearing, taste, smell, touch and a balance sense. At birth all the senses are in working order. What exactly can the infant perceive? We know that the senses of taste, touch and smell are well developed. In addition the newborn can hear a wide range of sounds. Indeed we have seen that they can hear while in the womb. Their ability to localise sound and their sensitivity to pitch and loudness improves over the first year of life.

VISUAL PERCEPTION

Sight or vision is a well-researched sense and we will look more closely at what we know about a child's capacity in this area. At birth infants can see but the visual apparatus is immature. The lens of the eye cannot change shape: it is fixed in such a way that clear, focused vision is possible at around 10 in. If you think about this distance you can see it has a significance. When feeding a baby at the breast, or close to you with a bottle, the baby can focus on the face of the mother, and we know that babies are interested in complexity and movement and enjoy looking at faces. As the baby develops so too does the eye. The nerve cells grow and increase, the fibres thicken to allow information to be carried more speedily and efficiently. This development occurs in all nerve cells during the early years. By the end of six months the baby's visual system functions much the same as that of the adult. When feeding, changing and bathing the baby one has a good opportunity to stimulate the various senses. By speaking in a quiet voice, smiling and looking at the infant one can develop a type of non-linguistic dialogue which acts as a precursor to later turn-taking and conversation.

FORM PERCEPTION

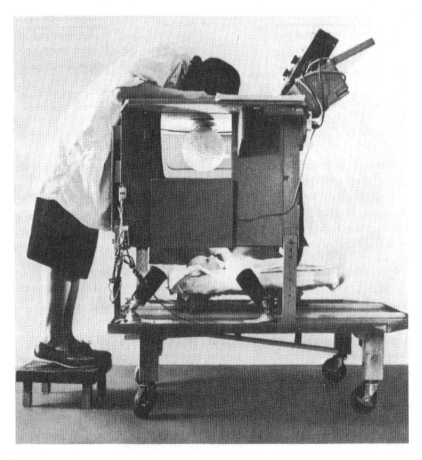

In studying what exactly babies can see, Robert Fantz developed a most intriguing test situation called the 'looking chamber'. The 'looking chamber' was designed like a cot. Fantz organised the sides of the cot in such a way that two cards — with varying patterns — could be displayed at the same time, one on either side. By observing the attention given by the babies to different patterns he discovered a great deal about the visual capacities of the young infant. In one test of thirty babies aged between one and fifteen weeks he showed them four different patterns. He noted that where one pattern was more complex in form than the other the babies would look at it for longer periods, suggesting a preference for complexity. It is argued that, as the babies were so young, it is unlikely that they had learned this preference and so a preference for complexity of form is considered an innate capacity, that is a capacity present from birth.

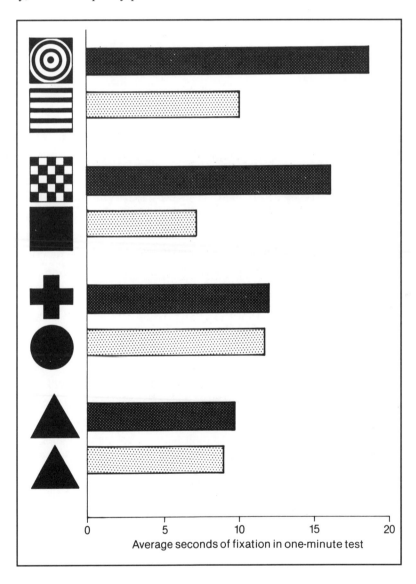

Using cards with black and white stripes paired with grey cards Fantz established that babies as young as six months can distinguish, at a distance of 10 in, stripes at $\frac{1}{64}$ inch apart as a pattern rather than a grey blur. Based on his earlier work he argued that babies will look at form in preference to a plain colour. Where they can perceive the detail they will look at the stripes for longer and in preference to the grey cards. This they did. This ability to distinguish detail, visual acuity, is not equal to an adult's visual acuity but does show a considerable ability at a young age. As babies get older their ability to perceive detail improves.

PERCEPTION OF THE HUMAN FACE

Is there an innate capacity in the newborn to respond preferentially to the human face? If there is it would make sense from an evolutionary standpoint in that it would promote social interaction and survival. Fantz argued, from his research, that babies do spend more time looking at a 'real' face pattern than a 'scrambled' face or a complex, non-facial pattern. He interpreted his results as supporting the theory that a preference for the human face is innate. Despite the fact that this may appeal to our logic his studies have not been replicated. That means that other researchers have failed to achieve the same results. By two months, when scanning is more mature and experience wider, babies do indeed spend more time regarding the 'real' face over the 'scrambled' face. It seems, therefore, that while the ability to pick out complexity of form is innate the ability to perceive the human face develops over time.

The development of facial perception during the first few months of life assists the infant's ability to recognise and respond to the expressive behaviour of others. The smile is an important expression and the social smile is an important aspect of attachment formation between babies and adults. By the middle of the second month — at about six weeks — infants smile at a variety of stimuli including the human face. Where the baby's smile is rewarded by a return smile, babies will smile all the more!

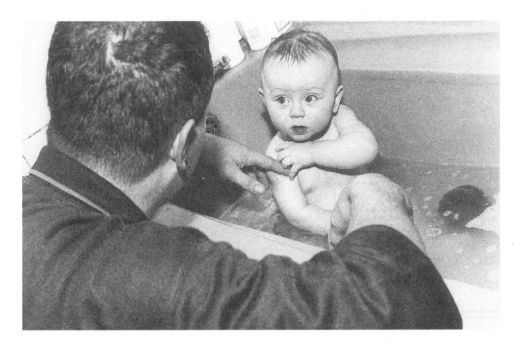

DEPTH PERCEPTION

Another area of perception that has interested researchers is that of the perception of depth. Research using the Visual Cliff (see diagram) suggests that by the time babies are able to crawl they can discriminate between deep and shallow surfaces. Gibson and Walk, in a classic experiment in 1960, placed babies on the Visual Cliff and observed their crawling pattern.

They were not inclined to crawl over the perceived drop suggesting that they had perceived the difference in depth. This does not tell us, however, about younger babies, as yet unable to crawl, and their abilities. Using a different procedure, measuring the heart rate of young infants who were placed on the shallow or deep side of the cliff, researchers were able to pick up a change in heart rate with a significant drop when the infant was placed on the deep side and little change when on the shallow side. This suggests that the young infants could discriminate the difference in depth between the deeper and the shallow sides.

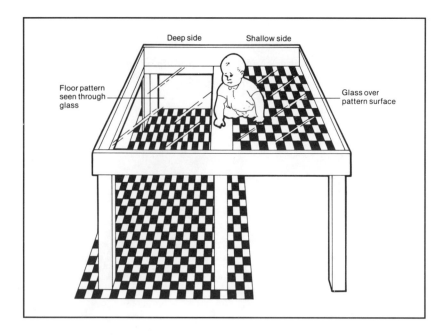

Deep side   Shallow side

Floor pattern seen through glass

Glass over pattern surface

From the first months of life until the age of about seven years a child's perceptual skills become more refined and her reactions and ability to note detail improve. This parallels the development of the ability to take in, sort and remember information which will be discussed in more detail in the chapter on thinking.

Accuracy of visual perception develops so that by the age of seven years a child can perceive, gather information and think about perceptual information in a way similar to an adult. Prior to this the child can make good visual discrimination but is impeded in using this information by her weakness in gathering, remembering and thinking about the information.

Perception is a prerequisite for learning. We learn in many ways: for instance we learn to continue behaving in a certain way when we are praised or rewarded; we learn to decrease behaviour that yields no response in others or that is punished. By observing others and by imitation we also learn a great deal. In all these procedures we use our ability to perceive. As adults working with young children it is important to recognise the capacities of the young child. Being aware of what they can do, even at a very young age, and how this might influence their behaviour and their learning, can inform practice and ensure that appropriate materials and opportunities are provided. Recognising that children are only developing the skills of perception and the ability to interpret their perceptions can also help adults understand the mistakes and misunderstandings that can arise in their interpretation of events.

SUMMARY

The neonate is a more competent individual than was once believed. She is born with a repertoire of organised behaviour patterns, reflexes, and all her senses are working to a certain degree.

Motor development improves remarkably over the first twelve months so that the infant develops from the immobile state of the early months to the mobility we see in the average twelve-month-old. Fine motor skills also emerge so that by nine months the baby can pick up a small object using the forefinger and thumb — the Pincer grasp.

The area of perception has been well researched, particularly that of visual perception. Robert Fantz developed a series of interesting experiments which showed how complex the young baby's visual skills are. They appear to be born with the ability to perceive form and they quickly develop the ability to perceive detail. Gibson and Walk, and later Bower, have shown that very young babies can perceive depth and distance.

Important to social development is an ability to perceive the human face and research also carried out by Fantz suggested that young babies show a preference for the human face. This has not been replicated by other research but we do know that by two months babies do show a particular interest in the human face.

The development of perception is linked to the ability to sort, order and remember information. For this reason children's competence in this area continues to develop until they reach the age of, approximately, seven years.

EXERCISES

1. What is meant by the 'competent' infant?

2. What is a reflex?

3. Select a partner and describe the Moro Reflex, the Rooting Reflex and the Babinski Reflex. Ask your partner to identify their value in relation to our understanding of child development.

4. Design a graph/table to illustrate how motor development progresses over the first twelve months.

5. Distinguish between the Palmer and Pincer grasp.

6. Describe the experiment by Fantz which suggests that babies are born able to perceive form.

7. What is the 'Visual Cliff'? What does it tell us about depth perception?

8. In a small group discuss how your knowledge of early perceptual and motor development might affect your practice when working with babies under a year old.

chapter 6
the development
of thinking

The development of thinking (cognitive development) is a process involving *perception, memory* and *concept formation.*

Perception: We have seen in the section on perception that the visual system of the infant is not fully developed. While able to see form shortly after birth the ability to perceive detail is less well developed. By four months the infant's ability to focus is as well developed as that of an older child, however, the infant's lack of experience does not allow her to recognise all she sees. Perception involves making sense of information. To make sense one must attend and concentrate and this is a skill young children develop over time. We know then that improvements in perception occur over time as a result of changes in the maturity of the perceptual system and as a result of experience. Perception has a profound effect on the efficiency of thinking.

Memory: To make use of information in thinking it must be retained and be accessible as necessary. We saw in the section on observation that, as a species, humans ignore a lot of information gathered through the senses. However, a great deal of information, often without our awareness, is actually stored in memory.

Very young babies can remember, they respond differently to different sights and by seven to nine months clearly recognise the difference between the familiar and the unfamiliar face exhibiting the characteristic Stranger Anxiety. This is where babies 'make strange' when lifted by, or even close to, an unfamiliar adult. The process is more one of *recognition* than of *recall*. Recognising something when it is presented is easier than recalling something when it is absent. Older children can recall things even when they are not there — such as a missing toy, a phone number, the layout of a room. The ability to recall develops through childhood, and children's interest in games, such as the card game 'memory', bears this out. Research has shown that for children and adults alike it is easier to remember things that are meaningful and linked rather than that which has no context at all. In experiments, lists of nonsense words are recalled less efficiently than real words as it is easier to link real words within a context and this facilitates recall. This is an important factor to remember when working with young children: the more meaningful you make the experience, the better value it will have for the child.

Concept Formation: There is so much information to store for the individual that it is beneficial and necessary to try and make information collection and storage as efficient as possible. This is rather like filing material away in alphabetic order rather than simply piling leaflets, letters, notes and bills all in one heap. Humans store information efficiently by grouping similar ideas and objects together to form what are called concepts.

- Concepts can be *concrete* — such as the concept of 'cup' or 'car' or 'animal'.

- Concepts can be *more specific* — such as 'mug/teacup' or 'citroen/ford' or 'horse/sheep'.

- Concepts can be *abstract* — such as the concept of 'happiness', 'justice' or 'society'.

The ability to form concepts, to think of things in terms of concepts, that is conceptually, improves with age. Language assists labelling which, in turn assists concept formation. As language develops children have names for concepts; these are not always accurate, however. My young daughter took to calling all small four-legged animals 'Sadie' after she had heard us call our black cat 'Sadie' and carried the concept far further than it holds. Gradually she recognised 'cat' as opposed to other four-legged animals and 'Sadie' as a name specific to one particular black cat. This over-extension of a concept when it is not clearly understood can account for the tendency of children to call all men 'fathers' and women 'mothers'. Before I had children of my own I used to be amused when young children would ask me where was my child, assuming that because I was an adult and female I was a 'mammy'.

Children can also make mistakes in their understanding of a concept. A neighbour's child, at almost three years of age, used to enjoy stroking our cats and we would caution her by saying 'gently, gently'. One day she came to me and said she wanted to 'gently' the cat! Clearly she had associated the word 'gently' with the act of stroking.

From even the slightest contact with young children it is clear that they do not think in the same way as adults. Their behaviour and conversations shed light on their incomplete grasp of the rules and the various understandable misunderstandings that they experience. Their ability to understand concepts, rules and ideas grows out of their experiences and develops as they mature. This issue of the development of reasoning, intellectual or cognitive development has been studied at length by development psychologists.

AN IMPORTANT NAME IN CHILD DEVELOPMENT

Jean Piaget is an important name in the history of studies into thinking. A brilliant man, he was interested in the origins of knowledge and how humans develop the ability to think. Piaget originally studied to become a biologist. He was born in Switzerland in 1896 and he studied zoology initially. He was interested in the various ways different animals adapted to their environments, how they grow and shed fur, live in a shell and so on. This idea of adaptation was to become basic to his later theory of cognitive development.

Turning to the human species, he became interested in how they adapted to their environments, discovering fire, wearing clothes, but more importantly, and unlike any other animals, how they changed the environment to fit their needs. He was particularly concerned to explain how the mental structures developed to allow the dependent child become an independent adult.

His early interest and work on thinking and the development of thought grew from his work in Paris where he worked on the standardisation of a French version of an English intelligence test. This exercise involved asking a wide variety of children of different ages and backgrounds a wide variety of questions of varying complexity. This is the method used to establish what questions the average child can answer or what problems they can solve at any given age. When the standardised test is finalised it can be used widely as a measure for comparing one child to the expected norm for her age. As well as recording details on questions answered correctly, Piaget also took account of the incorrect answers given. He noted the actual answer rather than simply recording it as a failure. This record of actual answers, particularly wrong ones, allowed him to identify a pattern to the wrong answers so that he began to realise that all five-year-olds were inclined to yield the same wrong answer to a particular question. By cataloguing the wrong answers he concluded that children do not think like adults. Rather all children exhibit a particular pattern of thinking which, by seven or eight, is similar to that of adults. He also concluded that this difference in thinking is not simply because they have less information or knowledge but because the way they handle the information varies from age to age in a predictable pattern.

Piaget returned to Switzerland and began to study the development of thinking. He considered that the mind — like the body — builds structures, which he called mental structures or *schema*, over the course of development. As these mental structures develop the child achieved a better ability to adapt to the world. For Piaget, cognitive development was the process whereby we each, actively, discover the nature of reality. We do not require any external reward: we are, he believed, motivated to develop from within.

In discussing intelligent behaviour Piaget considered it to be our ability to adapt. The theory he proposed was that **adaptation** involves the building up of schema through direct interaction with the environment. Adaptation is made up of two processes that are complementary. They are: **assimilation** and **accommodation**. We assimilate information and make it part of ourselves, to fit our current level of schema. We accommodate to information by changing our schema to take in new information. We alter our schema to accommodate to new information.

Adaptation = Assimilation + Accommodation

For example, a preschool child who sees her first camel at the zoo and calls it a horse has run through her collection of schema to find a fit. The camel is most easily assimilated as a horse. A preschool child who calls the same camel a 'lumpy horse' is beginning to become aware of the different properties of the camel and revises her schema to accommodate to the new information about the camel.

Adaptation, through assimilation and accommodation, is, according to Piaget, occurring at all times and adaptation leads to cognitive change as a result of direct contact with the environment. It happens less by being told what is the reality than by experiencing the reality through one's own active involvement in trying to understand the reality. Piaget's approach to studying this complex area was to observe very young children and interpret their behaviour in terms of the early stages of thinking. He would ask older children questions about their behaviour and beliefs and probe into the meaning behind their answers. He might ask 'Why does it rain' and listen carefully to the child's response and ask for clarification and explanation as the need arose. In this way he was able to explore how children were thinking about the world and how their current understanding could account for what other adults considered errors.

From his work Piaget concluded that children were not empty vessels or blank slates waiting to be filled with knowledge. They were, rather, actively involved in the construction of their understanding of the world. They sought rules to explain events:

'the sun is hot because there is a fire there'; 'big ships float because they are big'; 'small boats float because they are small'. They were not always logical or accurate in their explanations but it was through this active learning that they came to understand the world and this, he saw, as the development of intelligence. By carefully observing, talking to and listening to children he argued that one could come to understand how children understand their world.

STAGE THEORY OF COGNITIVE DEVELOPMENT

From his work Piaget identified four stages in the development of thinking. These stages occur in the same order in all children and are *invariant* — that is they must occur in the order outlined. The rate of appearance of the stages may vary from individual to individual and, indeed, from culture to culture but the pattern of the emergence of the stages stays the same. These stages are considered to differ in quality, that is to be qualitatively different from each other. At different ages children arrive at different understandings of the world. Action is the basis for the development and stimulation should be appropriate to the child's stage of development but sufficiently challenging to encourage development towards the next stage.

> **Piaget's stages of cognitive development**
>
> - From birth to about two years of age children go through the *sensori-motor period*.
>
> - From two to approximately seven years of age they go through the *pre-operational period*. It is called the pre-operational period as it precedes the onset of *operational* thinking — where thought is orderly and logical in character. This stage is subdivided into the *preconceptual* stage where a child's ability to form concepts is only emerging and the *intuitive* stage during which concept formation improves and children's guesswork is moving towards more adult type thinking — they have an intuitive grasp of logical concepts.
>
> - From seven to about eleven years of age children go through the *concrete operational* stage. Here thinking is becoming operational, more logical and organised. They are capable of concrete problem solving but still lack the facility with abstract concepts found in adult thinking. Math concepts, for example, are grasped through concrete experiences with blocks, beads, fingers and such like and it is not until the age of eleven or twelve that what used to be called 'mental arithmetic' becomes possible.
>
> - Finally Piaget identified the *formal operational* stage. This emerges from eleven years onwards. Here thought is logical, ordered and more abstract. Children can generate hypotheses and theories about the world and thinking is less bound by the concrete reality.

UNDERSTANDING YOUNG CHILDREN'S THINKING

For those working with young children the first two stages proposed by Piaget are of most importance and so we will look more closely at these. Understanding what happens during the development of thinking can help us explain much of children's behaviour and allows us to respond to them and plan for developmentally appropriate experiences.

Sensori-motor Stage: During this stage, as the name suggests, babies learn through their senses and their movements. As babies have limited language their concept formation (or preconcepts, really) develop through doing things. Observing young babies you will see them reach, touch, kick, push and pull at things. They finger objects, suck them, throw them and look closely at them. All these actions help the child establish herself as a separate being from the world around her. As the baby acts on the world she assimilates objects and events to her own schema and through experience accommodates to new objects and events. The baby is beginning to construct a model of the world, is developing more complex schema by building on her existing, more simple ones.

Two important capacities emerge during the sensori-motor period. These are *imitation* and *play*. Imitation, modelling or copying behaviour, is evident from the earliest months in a child's life. A baby sticks out her tongue, the adult repeats this as the baby watches and the baby imitates the adult. Later this skill develops so that towards the end of the period the child imitates actions, such as clapping or waving, and sounds, including those she makes herself in her babbling. Piaget sees imitation as a pure form of accommodation — the child puts all her effort into modifying her behaviour to fit in with what she perceives. Play, on the other hand, is, according to Piaget, predominantly assimilation. Here the child practises previously learned skills for the pleasure and fun of it.

Object permanence: The baby's earliest actions also help her to move towards an understanding that objects exist even when out of sight. Babies of four to five months, if their rattle goes missing or out of reach, do not search for it or try to reach it. Out of sight is, it appears, out of mind. Later, by seven to nine months, they will try to reach a fallen rattle. This can become a game where the baby throws the rattle to the ground, you pick it up and they throw it again and again. Piaget called this process the development of *object permanence* whereby children seem to be able to recall the existence of an absent object. He carried out some interesting experiments to test this process which are easily repeated.

Testing for object permanence:

> Take an eight-month-old; show her an attractive, colourful object; hide it under a cloth in full view of the infant — she will reach and remove the cloth to retrieve the object. This activity involves removing the cloth (*means*) to retrieve the object (*end*). This means-end behaviour is considered by Piaget to be one of the earliest intelligent actions and a foundation for later problem solving. However, even at this stage the child's sense of object permanence is limited. If, for example, the hidden object is moved to another location in a second situation the child will continue to search in the first location, under the cover, and show no interest in looking elsewhere. By twelve to eighteen months the child has developed a more advanced notion of object permanence and will search in different locations until she finds the object — evidence of growing problem solving behaviour, a measure of the development of thinking. Some research by Tom Bower suggests that babies may achieve object permanence by the fifth month and that this ability, like form discrimination, discussed in the previous chapter, may even be innate.

Towards the end of the sensori-motor period children begin to use symbols in their thinking and behaviour. The symbols we use most are words and by the middle of the second year — around eighteen months — most children have some clearly distinguishable words. Once they begin to use language their thinking moves from action-based thinking towards symbolic thinking. There is still a big difference between the thinking of a two-year-old and a ten-year-old but the onset of language and the move towards symbolic reasoning are important steps in the process of development.

Relating theory to practice: The experiences children have in the first two years of life are important to the way in which they develop through the sensori-motor period. It is essential that they have the opportunity to see, hear and do many different things. They should be carried about, placed in interesting locations around the room or the house, given appropriate toys and spoken to. The very young baby enjoys mobiles and the various objects that you can stretch in front of the pram, pushchair or baby seat. Even though babies can't talk they enjoy being spoken to and sung to. Evidence from babies who have spent their first years confined to cots in understimulated environments show that they suffer serious delay and their development is severely compromised.

> As children move towards the next stage of cognitive development you can observe the early stages of thinking, as we define it, in their actions. Take a child of eighteen months playing with a saucepan. She might take the lid off the saucepan and put it on and then take it off. This repetition is pleasing to her. Later she might fill the saucepan with blocks and try to put on the lid — it does not fit. She pauses, looks at the lid, the saucepan, the blocks and then empties out all the blocks. She places the lid onto the saucepan and it fits, she takes it off and fills the saucepan with the blocks again. She tries to fit on the lid, it does not fit. She repeats these actions a number of times and then it seems to dawn on her. She takes out a small number of blocks and then, with satisfaction at a problem solved, she fits on the lid. This episode illustrates the beginnings of thinking, problem solving.

PRE-OPERATIONAL PERIOD

From two to seven years of age Piaget identified the pre-operational stage. This has been characterised by a number of distinct features in the way children think about and interact with the world. Whereas the first stage of thought can be considered dominated by *action*, thought during the second stage could be said to be dominated by *perception* — that is children are easily influenced by the appearance of objects and events. You will be familiar with this from your own experience with children at this age. This is the period where men with white beards and red suits are really Santa Claus; it's the period where what is biggest is best, with children not wanting a broken biscuit but wanting the whole one and wanting the glass with the highest level of orange even if it is in a very narrow glass.

Pre-operational Thought in Action:

I saw an interesting example of how perception can dominate the thinking of young children. Some years ago a group of three to four-year-olds were being entertained by students at Christmas. During the course of a short play one student stood on the stage and put on a hat, a beard; later she pulled on a 'Santa' suit. All the children had observed the transformation and yet once she had the suit on she became Santa Claus. This was confirmed for me by the fact that as the children left the hall some ran back to Santa and explained what they wanted for Christmas.

A second feature of thinking at this stage is that children's thought *centres* on one element or detail of a situation and cannot easily take all the elements into account — they have difficulty in *decentering*. A classic series of experiments carried out by Piaget illustrates this.

PIAGET'S CONSERVATION STUDIES

Original Presentation	**Transformation**

Conservation of Liquid:

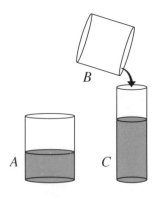

Is there the same amount of
liquid in each beaker?

Now is there the same amount
of liquid in each beaker?

Conservation of Mass:

Is there the same amount of
playdough in each ball?

Now is there the same amount of
playdough in each shape?

Conservation of Number:

Are there the same number
of sweets in each row?

Now are there the same number
of sweets in each row?

In the first, the child sits at a table on which there are three beakers, A, B and C. Beaker A is filled with a liquid — milk or orange juice. Beaker B — identical to A — is filled to the same level. The child acknowledges that both beakers contain the same amount of liquid. Beaker C is taller and narrower than beakers A and B. The liquid from B is poured, in full view of the child, into beaker C. Because of the nature of the beaker the liquid rises higher than that in beaker A. Older children, when asked, will agree that both beakers contain the same amount of liquid but Piaget found that younger children — younger than six or seven years — were, as it were, fooled by appearances and beaker C, with liquid at a higher level, was seen to contain more. Children under seven have difficulty in recognising that volume is conserved even where it changes in appearance. Piaget argued that their thinking is characterised by an inability to *conserve*.

He also carried out *conservation* experiments with objects such as buttons, sweets, plasticene/playdough. For instance, he presented a child with two identical balls of playdough. When asked, the children agreed that they were the same. Taking one he rolled it into a long snake-like shape. When asked the younger children indicated that they no longer contained the same amount of playdough. The visual information appears to be more powerful in guiding their thoughts than the logic of the situation.

A final illustration of this important characteristic can be seen in an experiment with sweets. As you would expect Piaget found that children under six were unable to conserve. When asked, they indicated that Row B2, in the diagram above, contained less sweets than Row A2, where the sweets had been spread out. This weakness in ability to conserve, this inability to decentre, to take account of more than one dimension in a situation, hinders the efficiency and accuracy of thinking in the pre-operational child.

If, however, you carefully remove the perceptual cues that interfere with the child's problem solving the child can exhibit conservation skills at an earlier age than predicted by Piaget.

In the example on page 100 children see the same actions as outlined earlier and they see the liquid being transferred from B to C. They are not, however, distracted by actually seeing the level of the liquids because this is hidden by the screen. This allows them to think about the problem posed without that interference of seeing two different levels of liquid. In such circumstances children at an earlier age can exhibit conservation. This suggests that Piaget's age estimates may underestimate the ability of children to think.

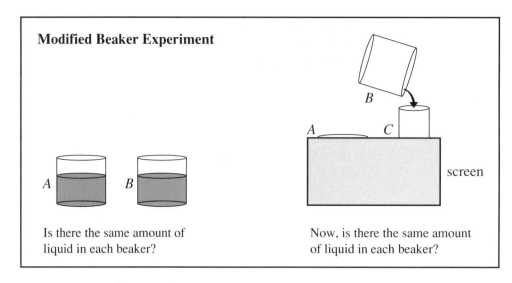

Modified Beaker Experiment

A *B*

Is there the same amount of
liquid in each beaker?

B

A *C*

screen

Now, is there the same amount
of liquid in each beaker?

Margaret Donaldson, author of the excellent book *Children's Minds*, and her colleagues at Edinburgh attempted to make some of the above experiments more 'child-friendly'. For instance, they introduced a 'naughty teddy' glove puppet into the sweets experiment described above and the puppet was seen to spread out the line of sweets. Children of four and five, younger than Piaget would predict, were able to explain that the 'naughty teddy' had moved the sweets and they indicated

that, despite the spreading out, there were still the same number as before. Thus when the problem is more carefully presented the younger child can conserve.

The Egocentric Child: From his observation and interviews with children during the pre-operational phase Piaget also concluded that they are more *egocentric* than adults. By this he meant that they have difficulty seeing things from another person's point of view. Once again you will have seen examples of this where, for example, a child tells you a story but assumes you know as much about it as she does. For instance three-year-old Sarah runs over to a visiting neighbour and says 'David didn't do it — it was John'. Because she knows who David and John are and is clear about what 'it' is she assumes that the adult (who like all adults may appear to know everything!) is also familiar with this information. She is unable to put herself in the adult's shoes. It can account for the fact that, for instance, saying to a three-year-old — 'don't hit her, how would you feel if she hit you? — has little or no effect. She simply cannot put herself in the position you suggest.

It is important to recognise that children find this difficult although, once again, research from Donaldson and her colleagues suggests that they may not be as egocentric as Piaget suggests. By presenting the same problems to children but in a more 'child-friendly' way they found them less egocentric than one would predict from the results Piaget found. This was illustrated in a study by Martin Hughes. He studied the 'three mountains' experiment carried out by Piaget. In this experiment Piaget had the child sit in front of a model of three mountains. On the top of one there was a cross, on the other a house and the third was directly in front of the child.

Among other things Piaget asked the child to describe, without moving, what a woman in the house on mountain No. 2 would be able to see from the window of the house. This proved a difficult task for younger children and their failure to succeed was interpreted as evidence of their egocentricity. Hughes, basing his study on the same principle, placed children in front of a different model. This model had two intersecting boards creating four rooms. From any position the child could only see two of the 'rooms' this created. He then asked children to hide a teddy from a 'policeman'. This required seeing the model from the perspective of the teddy and the policeman. Children were able to succeed at the task at an age much earlier than one would predict from Piaget's work, suggesting that they are not as egocentric as he suggested.

A further feature of pre-operational thinking is an inability to *reverse* thought. Reversibility refers to the ability to mentally go through the steps of reasoning to solve a problem and to reverse the direction of the steps and return to the beginning. We do this, for instance, in the following math problem: $2 + 3 = 5$, $5 - 3 = 2$.

Because pre-operational children have limited flexibility in their thought, their reasoning/thinking can appear quite flawed. They may make connections where none exist — 'My picture tore because John is crying' — and fail to make the connections between events which adults may see as obvious, for example, 'If you eat your dinner up you can have a treat.' Furthermore, children — and the younger the child the truer this is — sometimes equate thinking with doing: 'stand on a crack, break your mother's back'.

Because Piaget focused on the limitations of thinking in the pre-operational child we may inadvertently slip into considering the two to seven-year-old only in terms of what they cannot do. This is very easily done. It is not in the least valuable and may in fact lead to a situation where young children feel they are unable to do anything. This sense of failure may lead to a decreased likelihood of a child trying out new things or guessing or experimenting which, in turn, can limit their learning.

While recognising the limitations of thinking at this stage it is essential also to recognise the wealth of things children of two to seven *can* do. Responding to and providing for this will have a much more positive effect on their development in the long run. It is for this reason that we must develop the skill of objective observation — it will allow us to observe what children can do and to be guided by this.

WAS PIAGET RIGHT?

Piaget is an important researcher in the field of child development. His methodology, his observations and interviews and his identification of stages in the development of thought have all led to more research and greater enquiry into how children think and learn. As indicated above, more recent research suggests that Piaget underestimated the skills of young children.

The work of Margaret Donaldson and her colleagues at Edinburgh, has demonstrated that, for instance, young children are not as egocentric as Piaget suggested. If one presents a situation carefully and in a way that has a meaning for the child, she can take another's point of view much more effectively than you would expect from Piaget's results. Likewise, other researchers have found that babies may develop object permanence earlier than predicted by Piaget and that, if confusing visual information is excluded, children can conserve earlier also.

Piaget set us thinking about how children think. He also may have affected the way we plan for children. His emphasis on the individual child has tended to focus attention on the lone child rather than the social child. Humans are social and in planning for children we must take account of this social aspect of their nature. More recent research suggests that children may be more efficient and capable than he suggested. We must be aware of what children can do and be observant of each individual child we have contact with so that we can facilitate and further their development. If we rely too much on what we expect we may find that we underestimate ability, in which case children will become bored and frustrated. If we overestimate ability and expect too much from children they will experience failure and frustration.

INTELLIGENCE

Differences between individuals in terms of the cognitive skills can derive from their inherited potential and their environmental experiences. In comparing individuals we often refer to one as more intelligent than the other. This concept of intelligence is widely used but very difficult to define. Attempts to measure intelligence go back to the early years of the century. Intelligence tests have been developed in an effort to measure the Intelligence Quotient (IQ) of a person. These are tests which require children to carry out a variety of activities which require the application of perception, memory and conceptual skills. There are many varieties of IQ tests, but all test problem solving skills, comprehension, memory and visual-spatial understanding. Tests take account of various abilities and it is the pattern or profile of scores achieved that yield the individual IQ score.

Although often criticised as being simply a measure of a child's skill at IQ tests, rather than a measure of 'true' intelligence, they are a useful tool in research as they afford a common measure on which to compare children. In the earlier part of the century it was believed that IQ tests gave a fixed measure of an individual's intelligence and the IQ came to be a labelling system which has since fallen into disrepute. How you do on an intelligence test can depend on a wide variety of factors and now one is more likely to use the test as a general guide rather than to yield a specific IQ figure. They are helpful in identifying areas of strength and weakness but there are other factors, such as ability to cope, flexibility in thinking and so on, that go to make up the truly intelligent person. In different situations different strategies for success are necessary. Where a child has successfully adapted to their environment, it is fair to consider them intelligent in the wider sense of the word. Here intelligence is more like the broad notion of *adaptation* that Piaget used.

DEVELOPMENT OF CREATIVITY

Creative ability — unlike intellectual ability — has generated much less research and debate over the last century. An exact definition of creativity is difficult to achieve. Creative behaviour can be represented by:

- *creative process* — the ability to see new relations between ideas, a willingness to fantasise and imagine

- *creative product* — the production of original ideas or objects.

Although intelligence and creativity may be tenuously related, people considered creatively accomplished, are not identifiable from school records as being particularly bright. Studies suggest that creativity and intelligence refer to two different aspects of human ability. Taking this as the starting point researchers have begun to investigate what type of thinking is associated with creativity. In the 1960s Guilford investigated the existence of two different types of thinking — *convergent* and *divergent*. Convergent thinking involves the use of established or given information to arrive at a single correct answer, for example: Pot-Top; Nip-Pin; Keep- ? (Peek). Divergent thinking, on the other hand, moves in many directions from the given information and arrives at an answer where no one answer is necessarily correct. It is divergent thinking that is associated with creativity.

Creativity exercise:

Take a moment to complete the following tasks. Compare your answers with your colleagues' and discuss the results.

- How many things can you make with a tooth pick?

- How many uses can you find for a brick?

- How many things can you use a paper clip for?

Signs of creativity in preschool children have been the focus of interest for researchers, mainly because it is generally agreed that it is an area of development that should be fostered by those caring for and working with young children. Wallach (1985) and others have found that creative young children are more playful than other children, more erratic in their work, have a tendency to see the humorous side of things and are more likely to respond aggressively to frustration than other children. Pepler and Ross (1981) in their studies with preschool children found that providing divergent play materials — assorted, random shapes, for instance —encouraged children to play in a creative way. More convergent material such as form boards and jigsaws do not encourage creative play. In general creative children are found to be more self-confident and curious, independent in their behaviour and tolerant of ambiguity than their less creative peers. They are also non-conforming, open to unusual possibilities and persistent at tasks. Furthermore it is accepted that all children possess creative abilities to some degree and this can be developed under certain conditions.

In studies seeking background factors and environmental influences that may affect the emergence of creativity, Getzels and Jackson (1962) found that creative children tend to have parents who use a low degree of punishment, exert low pressure to conform, are non-intrusive, are satisfied with and like their children and have a good sense of self-esteem. Recognising these factors can assist other adults working with young children to provide a similarly supportive and positive atmosphere. Clearly a child-centred approach to early childhood services is more likely to yield an increase in creative behaviour than adult-dominated services allowing, as they do, for curiosity to be satisfied by the active involvement of the child.

Sometimes, in an effort to encourage children's creativity, adults can go to a lot of trouble preparing outlines of objects and animals, cutting different shapes in different colours and textures and preparing and planning specific art/creativity activities. Caution has been expressed about the value of sticking screwed-up tissue paper on to adult-prepared templates. Curtis, in her book *A Curriculum for the Preschool Child*, points out that all the children do in such situations, for example — filling in an outline snowman, colouring in a spider or a Valentine heart — is to follow adult direction. They don't, as it were, own the work. If adults invest too much time in organisation, preparation and direction they may end up stifling the creative urge in the child and possibly even lead to a sense of hopelessness — 'I'll never get this right'. Adults must trust that children will represent their world, through various media, at an appropriate developmental level, not always as adults might see it.

MORAL DEVELOPMENT

As children's thinking becomes more logical and efficient so too does their sense of right and wrong. Young children under seven have a poor grasp of right and wrong.

Moral development — how humans come to understand the difference between their selfish needs and their obligations to act in favour of the needs of others — is closely tied into cognitive development. Thinking about what is moral does not guarantee that people will behave accordingly. Moral behaviour can be influenced by outcome, circumstances and by personal emotions.

As children come to understand the purpose and function of co-operative social arrangements — such as sharing and turn-taking — they develop increased respect for rules and arrangements. The important point here is that children *come* to understand. You cannot force them to understand. By being clear and realistic in your rules and expectations you can assist the development of moral reasoning. However, expecting a one-year-old not to spill her food or accusing a three-year-old of being bold because she gets frustrated at a complex puzzle is of little value to either adult or child.

With cognitive maturity and broadening social experiences, children's concept of justice and fairness becomes more abstract. To study the development of moral understanding Piaget presented a series of stories to children of different ages. The stories were presented in pairs and related to different situations. Piaget would question the children about who, in the stories, was naughtiest and why. Here is an example of the stories used.

PIAGET'S STORIES

> • Story A: A little boy who is called John is in his room. He is called to dinner. He goes into the dining room. But behind the door there is a chair, and on the chair there is a tray with fifteen cups on it. John couldn't have known that there was all this behind the door. He goes in, the door knocks against the tray, bang go the fifteen cups, and they all get broken!
>
> • Story B: Once there was a little boy whose name was Henry. One day when his mother was out he tried to get some jam out of the cupboard. He climbed up onto a chair and stretched out his arm. But the jam was too high up and he couldn't reach it and have any. But while he was trying to get it he knocked over a cup. The cup fell down and broke.
>
> (Piaget, 1932/65, p. 22.)

From the responses he received to this and other stories about right and wrong Piaget identified two stages of moral development. The first, and earliest, he called *heteronomous* morality and the second stage he called *autonomous* morality. Heteronomous suggests a morality under the authority of others, adults.

Autonomous indicates a move towards a morality under the authority of the individual herself.

In the earlier phase typical of children from five up to ten years (in certain instances), the rules of right and wrong are regarded as unalterable and coming from all-powerful adults in the child's world. Here the intention behind an action is not given due regard in assessing its 'rightness' or its 'wrongness'. Rather the size of the damage or the degree of punishment directs the child in her judgment. So, for example, in the case of John who rushes into the room when called to lunch and knocks against a tray of cups breaking them all, younger children will consider him to be bolder than Henry who breaks one cup when trying to steal the jam. The size of the damage dictates the 'rightness' or 'wrongness' in the heteronomous stage and not the intention behind the action.

When assessing the measure of right and wrong in the above stories older children will take account of intention in judging the situation. They will find Henry to be bolder as he was doing something that he should not have been doing. The *intention* behind an act becomes important when judging it as right or wrong. At the autonomous stage rules are seen as flexible, socially negotiated instruments derived for the benefit of social co-operation.

Subsequent research has supported Piaget's broad view of a pattern to moral development. The work of Laurence Kohlberg has extended his work and identified the complexities of moral development. Kohlberg adapted Piaget's idea of the stories but he presented children and adults with a dilemma to study. He followed this with a series of searching questions to seek an understanding of the level of moral reasoning in different individuals.

KOHLBERG'S HEINZ DILEMMA

In Europe a woman was near death from a very special kind of cancer. There was one drug that the doctors thought might save her. It was a form of radium that a druggist in the same town had recently discovered. The drug was expensive to make, but the druggist was charging ten times what the drug cost him to make. He paid £200 for the radium and charged £2,000 for a small dose of the drug. The sick woman's husband, Heinz, went to everyone he knew to borrow the money, but he could only get together about £1,000, which is half of what it cost. He told the druggist that his wife was dying, and asked him to sell it cheaper or let him pay later. But the druggist said 'No, I discovered the drug and I'm going to make money from it'. So Heinz got desperate and broke into the man's shop to steal the drug for his wife. Should Heinz have done that? Why? (from L. Berk's *Child Development*, p. 522)

From his work Kohlberg identified six stages of moral development rather than the two proposed by Piaget. He grouped these stages into three levels of moral reasoning which he called *Pre-Conventional, Conventional* and *Post-Conventional*. Up to the age of seven, children are really considered pre-moral. They respond to simple rules, but their understanding of why is based more on the expected consequences than a true understanding of justice and fairness. Moral reasoning moves from this basic level through to a rule-based morality where the rules of the state, religion and society are taken as the base for judging right and wrong. The higher order moral reasoning takes account of intention and social responsibility. For a good discussion on this area see *Moral Development* by R. Duska and M. Whelan.

The development of self-control — an aspect of emotional development and an important aspect of socially appropriate behaviour — is influenced by cognitive and representational capacities that emerge during the second year of life. Children as young as two years have been found able to use self-directed speech to await a wanted consequence (waiting until after dinner for a sweet 'I'll eat my dinner and then have my sweet'). Where provided by adults with clear, unambiguous strategies (rules) for a small, identified number of wanted behaviours, the preschool child can be helped behave as appropriate in the given situation. In some cases a child only comes to recognise a rule by breaking it, or where there is an inconsistency in the consequences of particular behaviours: yesterday you could not stand on the chair to reach the book and were 'given out to'; today you are told to stand up on the chair and get the book yourself! Where children are unclear about expected behaviour it is more likely that management and discipline problems will emerge.

Understanding the process of moral development helps us ensure that our practice with young children respects them. It encourages us to provide for them in a way that assists their journey towards moral maturity rather than demanding of them behaviour which they are too young to understand. Believing in the child, respecting her and, in so far as possible, understanding her developmental progress, yields practice that is rewarding and less stressful for the adult and that is positive, encouraging and empowering for the child.

SUMMARY

'Cognitive' is the term used to describe the development of thinking or reasoning. The process, cognition, depends on perception, memory and concept formation. Concepts can be concrete — cup; more specific — China teacup, or abstract — happiness. Language assists us in the development of concepts and improves the effectiveness and efficiency of thinking. Many misunderstandings can be explained in terms of children's poor conceptual understanding.

Jean Piaget was a most influential figure in the unfolding of our understanding of the process and pattern of cognitive development. He argued that human beings adapt to their environment and he saw this process as one of adaptation. He proposed the following equation to explain the process: Adaptation = Assimilation + Accommodation.

Piaget identified four stages of cognitive development and their order is *invariant*. The stages are called:

- Sensori-Motor Period
- Pre-operational Period — Preconceptual
                                 — Intuitive
- Concrete Operations
- Formal Operations.

From his work he identified different characteristics in children's thinking. More recent research by Margaret Donaldson and her colleagues in Edinburgh, among others, have repeated Piaget's work and modified it somewhat to become more 'child-friendly'. Their work suggests that Piaget may have underestimated the capacities of young children.

The term intelligence is difficult to define and is related to what Piaget called adaptation. One can compare individuals in terms of their intelligence by comparing their scores on intelligence tests. These tests give a measure called the Intelligence Quotient (IQ).

Creative development is a process that occurs in all humans although certain people are more creative than others. Researchers have identified certain characteristics common to creative children and have also found that there are common styles in the parenting of such children. Guilford found two types of thinking which he called *Convergent* and *Divergent*. Divergent thinking is associated with creative thought. Results of research can assist adults in encouraging creativity in young children.

The process by which children come to understand concepts such as right and wrong is known as moral development. Moral development is closely linked to cognitive development. Piaget and Kohlberg have both contributed to our understanding of children's moral reasoning.

Understanding the process of cognitive development can assist adults in interpreting children's behaviour and responding appropriately to their needs.

EXERCISES

1. Write brief notes on any two of the following:

   • Cognitive development

   • Concept formation

   • Moral development

   • Creativity

2. What was Piaget's main contribution to our understanding of children's thinking?

3. What do the terms: Adaptation, Assimilation and Accommodation mean? How are they related to each other?

4. List the four stages of reasoning identified by Piaget.

5. Write a short essay about the characteristics of children's thinking during the pre-operational stage (two to seven).

6. What are the main criticisms of Piaget's work?

7. How can your knowledge of creative development, and the factors affecting it, contribute to your practice with young children?

8. How are cognitive and moral development linked?

chapter 7
language development

We lay a lot of emphasis on language development as a measure of general development. When parents meet with young children of the same age you will often hear questions such as 'Does she talk much yet?' or comments like 'She's got a lot of words' or 'She's very quiet isn't she?' As well as being of interest to parents the process of language development has attracted the attention of psychologists, speech therapists and all those working with young children. Many researchers into language development have studied the structure of language and the rules of grammar with particular emphasis on understanding how young children come to be able to speak so fluently at such an early age. Other research has focused on mother/infant and adult/child interactions and has recorded the type of language that occurs. Results from this type of research can give useful guidelines for practice to those whose responsibility it is to care for and educate young children.

Language is a form of communication and when we talk of language we generally mean spoken or verbal language. There are, of course, other forms of communication such as gesture, tone of voice, body position and so on. Even very young children pick up on aspects of this non-verbal communication and older children recognise where there is a mis-match between what is said and the accompanying non-verbal messages. The overtired mother, asked for sweets, who says — in a very particular tone of voice — 'I'll give you sweets!', really means that there is no chance that sweets will be given and beyond a certain age children recognise this. The clue to the meaning of this sentence is in the tone of voice rather than the words spoken, that is, it is a non-linguistic clue to meaning. Use of tone of voice and facial expression can give the listener much information about the real meaning behind words.

This chapter will refer primarily to the development of spoken language, but reference will also be made to non-verbal communication and elsewhere in the book to other means of communication, such as music, drama and art.

In studying language development there are three main questions we need to answer :

1. What is the course of language development?

2. How does a child learn language so well in so short a space of time?

3. How can this information help me in my work with young children?

These questions will be dealt with in detail throughout this chapter, but briefly:

What is the course of language development? There are identifiable stages in language development and an understanding of the pattern can help you evaluate a child's language development, provide a stimulating, enriched environment and enjoy talking with the young child. While research indicates a clear pattern of language development, it is important to remember that the rate of passage through language development will vary considerably from child to child. This is true even within one family. In my own case my children showed quite different rates; two daughters achieved precise and well-articulated language in the second year of their lives whilst a third daughter was slower to talk and more creative and experimental with her early language. Had I been unaware of the variability in 'normal' language development I could have been unnecessarily worried about her language development. Some of the factors which influence rate will be discussed later.

How does the child learn language so well in so short a space of time? This question is one that has interested researchers and has led to the search for a theory to explain this uniquely human characteristic. Are we born equipped to acquire language according to a particular timetable? Do we learn by imitation? Is there a time during which we *must* learn language? How much does our experience of language influence our language development?

How can this information assist me in my work with young children? Having answered the above questions we should be in a good position to look at language interaction, to listen carefully to what children say and to be more careful in how we speak to and with children. There is some concern that children cared for in group day-care may be at a disadvantage to children cared for at home in the early years, because they lack the one-to-one relationship that children at home may have. How can we, from what we know about language development, ensure that children get the very best language environment in a comfortable and relaxed atmosphere? What skills do adults need to develop and what planning is necessary for the different age groups and different abilities?

LANGUAGE DEVELOPMENT

In order to talk, children must have developed other skills such as listening and attending to aspects of spoken language. You will recall that when discussing prenatal development it was noted that by the sixth month of pregnancy the mother may notice that the foetus reacts to loud noises by a startle movement. This indicates that even before birth human beings are equipped with necessary organs for hearing. So, before ever a child utters her first word, somewhere around the twelve to eighteen months, she has had a lot of exposure to sound and indeed has reacted to sound and communicated with others in different ways. You will recall that when we discussed perception we mentioned studies on young infants that show a remarkably high degree of ability in perceiving sounds. In one study, for example, it was found that babies can discriminate between sounds like 'b' and 'p' at a few weeks old. The method used was observing the sucking response to new sounds and it was found that having listened to the sound 'b' for a time the children stopped sucking and appeared to become disinterested. However, when the 'p' sound was introduced they resumed sucking with interest, showing their interest in novelty and their ability to recognise a novel sound. Also important to the development of language is the child's own interest and ability to communicate. This is evident in body language and gesture, even before the child is making sounds that are recognisably part of our language repertoire.

The period before a child begins to speak is called the *pre-linguistic* period. This period can be subdivided into different sections which I will call the *cry* stage, the *coo* stage and the *babble* stage.

The cry stage refers to the very earliest sounds made by the young infant and includes the spluttering, snuffling and cry sounds that are part and parcel of the breathing pattern of the very young child. The cry is a strong form of communication in which the child indicates her needs such as when hungry, wet, tired, uncomfortable or in need of company. The cry of the infant has been studied in great detail and research suggests that some mothers can clearly distinguish between a hunger and a pain cry. In some children, however, the cries can merge and it is difficult to tell them apart. Do cries tell us anything about language? There does not appear to be any difference between the cry of an Irish baby and that of an American, French or Japanese baby. Tape recordings of cries from infants of different nationalities have been analysed and no significant differences have been found.

115

Crying is considered pre-linguistic because — even though it is far removed from language — it does require the use of vocal organs and the control of the movement of air — a necessary prerequisite to speaking. Also a baby develops the pattern of cry, listen, attend — a definite precursor to the speak, listen, attend and respond.

The coo is a contented sound made by the young baby when she is fed, warm, dry and generally comfortable. It is an important stage on the way to language development because it encourages verbal interaction and the development of turn-taking between the baby and the carer. By this I mean that adults respond to a cooing, gurgling baby by talking to her, tickling her and generally allowing a form of conversation. Take, for example, this sample record:*

Mother:	Hello. Give me a smile (gently pokes infant ribs).
Baby:	(Yawns)
Mother:	Sleepy, are you? You woke up too early today.
Baby:	(Opens fist)
Mother:	(Touching infant's hand) What are you looking at? Can you see something?
Baby:	(Grasps mother's finger)
Mother:	Oh, that's what you wanted. In a friendly mood, then. Come on give us a smile.

*Recorded by Catherine Snow and reproduced by Sylva and Lunt

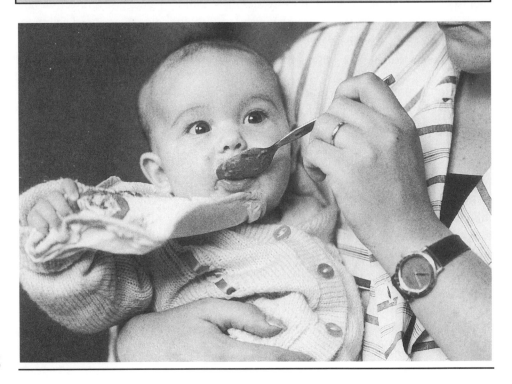

In this exchange you can see the conversational style being modelled by the mother for the baby. Even though the infant does not talk back she does get the opportunity to interact, the mother pausing to allow this. With very young children it is essential that this type of experience is given. If it is not, the child will simply stop interacting and not develop the turn-taking skills necessary for conversation and discourse.

The babbling stage is where the baby begins to make identifiable sounds. It is typified by the idea of the 'goo-goo' that you sometimes see in cartoons. This is not far from the truth as the early babbling sounds are consonants 'g' and 'k' and then the 'a', 'b', 'f' and 'd' sounds. It is of interest to note that the first word-like sounds made by infants throughout the world are more likely to be similar to the 'father' sounds of 'da-da' rather than the mother sounds of 'ma-ma'! An interesting fact, given that it is generally the mother with whom children are in most contact in these early years.

Babies begin to babble at around six months. They play with sounds, initially repeating the same pattern and gradually repeating mixed patterns such as 'babagagababa'. As this progresses intonation enters their babbling so it seems conversational. To encourage this development adults must talk to the babbling infant, who will happily attempt to imitate. As babbling develops there is a move from simple vocal play with sounds to the more melodic babbling of the baby at around nine months. There are some important characteristics of babbling; for instance all babies babble, even those who are deaf and do not hear sounds. With deaf babies, however, the babbling does not differentiate as a child develops and the melodic babbling of the later period does not appear. It also appears that all babies can make all the possible sounds of all languages and only gradually begin to show a preference for their own language sounds as they move towards eight or nine months. So, an Irish baby can babble sounds necessary for speaking in French, Japanese or German.

Babbling is not language but it does develop as a form of communication and in the later stages children babble in a conversational way with pauses, intonation and tone evident. Indeed parents often say, at this stage, 'Oh, you really want to talk, don't you?'

A language-rich environment, where the child's babbling is responded to and she is spoken to and hears conversation is important to future language development. Where studies have been done on institutionalised infants it is clear that their language, along with other aspects of their development, have been severely delayed. This is thought to be the result of lack of language stimulation resulting from the situation where various adults are responsible for caring for the infants on a physical level, but are not inclined to talk or chat with them as parents at home or carers in good quality settings would.

One clear factor emerges from our overview of the pre-linguistic phase and that is the *social* nature of communication. Humans are social beings and respond to human contact. In order to encourage and facilitate language development adults must be sociable with infants. We must talk to them, include them, allow them space, respond to them and above all attend to them. In this way their pre-linguistic experiences will lay a good foundation for the development of skills necessary to the next stage in language acquisition — the first word.

Games of give-and-take, such as peek-a-boo, ride-a-cock-horse, horsey-horsey and so on, help babies acquire the skill of turn-taking and by twelve to thirteen months they will slot words into places where actions had previously been. The familiar games, action songs and rhymes, such as round-and-round-the-garden and pop-goes-the-weasel, all encourage turn-taking, anticipation and joy. Through this the child is laying the foundation for future conversational skills. It is, therefore, important to set aside time with babies to allow for this type of play.

THE FIRST WORD

The 'da-da' and 'ma-ma' sounds from the babbling period are often mistaken for the child's first word. In fact we respond to these sounds as though they were words but a careful observation of the young child's use of these sounds will show you that they are used for a wide variety of objects and actions. Such sounds lack the essential characteristic of a word, that is that the sound should *consistently* refer to a specific object/person or action. Babbling is where the child is playing with sounds. Words, on the other hand, are planned, controlled speech.

The child will produce her first word somewhere between the twelfth and the eighteenth month but it can be earlier or later. This is a point worth stressing here. The age at which words appear can be quite varied and generally bear no relation to the overall intelligence or ability of the child. If, however, a child of two-and-a-half years is not using words then it is important to check out the possible reason for the delay. One cannot over-stress how important it is to recognise, however, the wide variation in achieving the first word because we do seem to lay a lot of emphasis on talking as a developmental milestone.

Over the years researchers studying first words have looked at the following questions: How much do children say? What do they say? How much do they understand? These questions can really best be taken together. Children initially use only one or two words and gradually build up, over time, to a vocabulary of about 200 words by the age of two years.

RATE OF VOCABULARY ACQUISITION

Birth	no words
6 months	babbling sounds but no real words
12 months	simple wordlike sounds 'mama, dada, gaga'
2 years	emerging two word sentences; vocabulary of 200 words
3 years	child experiments with language rules; 1,000 words
4 years+	grammar adult-like; full and varied vocabulary of over 2,000 words
Adults	most adults have an 'active' vocabulary of 4–5,000 words.

Researchers have studied the words that children produce in the beginning and, not surprisingly, a large percentage of words used are nouns referring to familiar objects. Words such as 'milk', 'bottle', 'car'. However, they are not always pronounced as adults pronounce them. So, for instance, a child may say 'bokkle' or 'tar'. Their production of the word is still immature. It is an interesting fact that even though they may pronounce the word incorrectly they recognise the correct pronunciation! My two-year-old daughter wanted the 'gool'. At first I was at a loss to understand her and repeated 'gool — do you want to go to school?' and made other such attempts to understand her. She persisted with 'No, goooool!' until I realised she meant the 'glue'. Although she called it 'gool' she would only accept my saying 'glue'! This is a common feature of young children's language.

Early words generally refer to the familiar and the 'here-and-now' in the child's world. It is, however, possible to group them into types and this is useful if you want to get a clear picture of a particular child's language. One suggested grouping is:*

People:	Relatives such as *mummy* or *baby* and can also include other familiar people.
Actions:	Words associated with action routines — *bye-bye, night-night* or *all-fall-down.* Single action words or verbs — *go, sit down, kiss,* and *say.*
Food:	*Milk* and *juice* or *drink(dink);* also words such as *nana(banana)* or *dindin.*
Parts of the Body:	First words of this category tend to refer to the face, e.g. *nose, mouth, eyes* and later to the limbs such as *leg* and *hand.* This category also includes reference to body functions such as *wee-wee* and *pooh.*
Clothing:	This includes word such as *nappy, diess (dress), shoes, coat.*

Animals:	The number of words in this category will depend on exposure, a child living on a farm will, for instance, have a wider selection than the child who has had no close contact with animals. Nonetheless, probably because picture books abound with pictures of animals this is a well filled-out category. Words here include *doggie, pussy, bird(ie) cow (moomoo)* and so on.
Vehicles:	*Car, bus, train* are typical early words. Children also refer to vehicles by their sound, so, for example, in Ireland a child will often refer to an ambulance as a *beebaw*.
Toys:	*Ball, book, dollie* are common words in this category but there will be variation as a result of different experiences.
Household objects:	The words here reflect that which is important in the daily routine; *bokkle (bottle), cup, bowl, poon (spoon).* Here objects may also be referred to by their sound such as *tick-tock* for clock.
Locations:	The words here are simple words of location such as *when, in, on* and *look.*
Social words:	Some parents stress the words in this category more than others. Words include *please, thank you, yes* and *no*.
Describing words:	In later language children produce words which we call adjectives such as *hot, dirty, big*.
'Empty' words:	These words have little meaning in their own right, because their meaning can change from situation to situation. An example is the word *him*; you know it refers to some male individual (although with young children even this may not be true as there is confusion between male and female referents) but you have no idea who. When you see who the child is pointing to, however, this 'empty' word gets a meaning. These are actually very important words and when accompanied with gestures can impart a lot of information and improve communication.

*From D. Crystal's *Listen to your child*.

EXPRESSIVE AND RECEPTIVE LANGUAGE

All speech is characterised by two aspects.

1) What is *understood*

2) What is *said*.

The first type of language is called *receptive* language and refers to language that the child understands. Children understand a lot more than they say and adults can be heard to say of a particular child 'She understands everything you say!' This, of course, is not the case but children do indeed understand a great deal more than they can say.

You can check a child's level of understanding by asking her to do specific things. With the young child you should only ask her to do one thing at a time, for example 'Close the door' or 'Bring me the cup' or to show you something, for instance, 'Show me the book' or 'Where's the dolly?' Where children are slow to talk, tests used to establish a possible cause will look very carefully at the level of receptive language. It is impossible to estimate how much speech an individual child understands. However, the more varied the language a child hears and the wider the vocabulary she is exposed to the better her general language development.

The second type of language is called *expressive* language and refers to the words that the speaker can say and use. Children move from an expressive language of some single words at about twelve months to 200 words at about two years and up to 2,000 words by their fourth year. This represents a type of explosion in language development in a relatively short space of time. The child's vocabulary multiplies and her interest in words, sentences, meaning and conversation all develop rapidly. It is a period that is exciting, if tiring, to observe and one where children enjoy talking and being spoken with; a period to enjoy. The type and amount of words and the quality of a child's expressive language will depend on such factors as hearing good quality conversation, being included in conversation and being guided and stimulated in her interest in words and talking.

A noticeable feature of children's first words is the tendency to *over-extend*. This refers to the case where one word can mean a wide variety of things. You will recall how our eldest child found 'Sadie' (the name of our cat) an easy word to say and over-extended the use of the word to mean any cat or dog, real or a toy — any small four-legged animal was a 'Sadie'. This gradually narrowed, with experience, to refer to black cats and finally it became the specific referent to our own cat. Adults may also use over-extension; in animals, for instance, to those of us not all that familiar with birds we may well call the 'rook', 'jay', 'hooded crow' and 'common crow' simply 'crows'.

Interestingly, as with pronunciation, the child will show over-extension in *production* but not necessarily in *comprehension*. Sylva and Lundt quote an example of a child faced with several objects he himself called 'apple' (some of which were not apples). When requested he was able to point to the correct drawings. So although in his production of speech he called all the objects 'apples', he was able to identify, let us say, the 'ball', 'balloon' and 'apple'.

Most adults naturally assist children in coming to discriminate between objects. For example, where a child might use the word 'butterfly' for all small insects, including flies, moths and daddy-long-legs an adult would say 'Yes, it is like a butterfly, isn't it — it's called a fly'. One doesn't need to correct the child or labour the point of their error. Indeed too much correction could well damage the child's fluency and inhibit her tendency to talk. Adults must be careful not to be too demanding of correct pronunciation, after all it is communicating the message that is important. Similarly adults ought to avoid highlighting children's tendencies to error. While this is often done with the best of intentions children do not like to feel humiliated or laughed at any more than adults do and can pick this up even where it may not be intended. So, if a child uses or pronounces a word in a particularly 'cute' way relish the moment, but do not force the child to repeat the word or attempt to show her off to others.

SENTENCE FORMATION

Once the child has attained a vocabulary of single words we can begin to identify what are called *holophrases*. A holophrase is a one-word sentence. For example, if a child says 'gone' it can mean a variety of things depending on the context in which the word is used; it may mean 'my milk is gone', 'Daddy is gone to work' or 'there is no more playdough'. It is important to listen to the child carefully, observe gesture and take account of the context in which the child speaks if you are to understand what she is trying to say. Listening to children is also modelling an appropriate conversational behaviour and helps them develop the listening skills so important to communication.

Early Sentences: As the child becomes more confident with using words, short sentences begin to emerge. The first sentences are two-word sentences and the meaning is usually clear from the context. These early sentences have been labelled *telegraphic speech*. This is an appropriate name because these sentences, just like the old style telegram, contain only the most important pieces of information. In adult speech a lot of content can be considered redundant to the specific meaning underlying the communication. You will be aware of how a good deal of meaningful communication can occur between, say, an Irish and a French man, although neither can speak the language of the other. Single words, short phrases, gesture and tone of voice all assist in getting the meaning across. Similarly with the early sentences of the young child. For example, take the sentence 'Daddy is gone to work'. Taking this particular sentence the young child may say 'Daddy goneh work'; she will not say 'Daddy is to.' In their early sentences all children appear able to pick out the key words, the essential meaning, and only later do they add in what are called the functor words of 'is' and 'to' in the above sentence.

Word order: Also notice the word order. You will see that the order is similar to that in adult speech. It may seem that through listening to speech in conversations around them children have picked out rules or grammar of the language and that they use these rules as they feel appropriate. However, this use of rules may be innate, a point to which we will return. Sometimes this use of rules gives rise to errors and indeed there are common errors observable when listening to the speech of children of the same stage of language development. Young children will say 'I goed to Nana's'; here they have identified the rule that past tense is created by the addition of '-ed' to a word, e.g. 'call', 'called' or 'walk','walked' but are not aware of the cases where this rule will not apply. A similar situation arises with plurals, the rule identified being to add an 's' to a word and so children will talk about the 'mouses' and 'womans' instead of 'mice' and 'women'. It has been found that this is common to all children acquiring language. Research has shown that this rule application is also applied to nonsense words. Young children were first shown a picture of, for instance, a 'wug'; they were then shown a picture of two wugs and asked what they saw. They replied 'wugs', showing their application of the plural rule.

EXTENDING CHILDREN'S LANGUAGE

In conversation with a child at this stage adults often extend her sentence and this can be very helpful. Recently on a bus I heard the following short interchange between a young mother and her child of about two-and-a-half years:

Mother:	Look at the water
Child:	Doohy waher
Mother:	Dirty water.

Here we see a short extension of the child's language sharpening the pronunciation of the words. There is room here for further extension such as 'Yes, the water is dirty'. One does need to be careful however and not over-extend and confuse or bore the child. Where a child mispronounces they are often aware of this. Indeed research has found that if you tape a three-year-old and play back the recording they have difficulty understanding themselves. However, if you play a recording of an adult saying the same thing with correct pronunciation they will understand. Crystal, in his book *Listen to your Child*, gives a rather nice example of a young boy, David, who says he is going on the 'mewwy-go-wound'. He is teased by his older sister who says 'Oh! David wants to go on the mewwy-go-wound'. A frustrated David says 'No! You don't say it wight.'

There is little point in correcting a child's pronunciation at this stage — you want, rather, to encourage conversation and sentence production. If, for instance, you stop a child mid-sentence to correct a word, it is likely that the child will lose her train of thought and may begin to avoid talking to you. You will, in fact, inhibit language development. Some people can be quite intolerant of poor pronunciation and consider a child as 'lazy' or 'bold'. This is of no value to the child; if there is a specific problem with general articulation, careful and sensitive handling is necessary.

Because of their relative immaturity with language children may misunderstand adult speech. Here it is important for us, as adults, to be aware of the words we use. As adults we are familiar with different turns of phrase, or different uses of words in different contexts. Not so the young child. For example:

| Mother: | You run on ahead, I'll catch up with you |
| Child (2.6): | Whose head, Mummy? |

| Mother: | Don't argue. |
| Child (3.0): | I don't argme. |

Children may also have difficulty with the use of particular words as in this example:

Child (5.2):	Is there any ice-cream around my lips?
Mother:	No, not that I can see.
Child (smiling):	That's why I licked it all off.

Here the child confuses the word 'why' and 'because'.

THE EVOLUTION OF THE QUESTION

As the child reaches the age of three there is a growth in the questions she includes in her conversation. Questions follow a clear pattern of development as follows:

- **Stage 1:** Children show signs of wanting to ask questions as early as the end of the first year and, changing their tone of voice, may say 'dada?'

- **Stage 2:** During the second year children start to use the question words what, where, and when, for example 'where the teddy?' or 'what a ye doin'?' Despite their interest in asking questions they may not always understand a question.

- **Stage 3:** By the beginning of the third year sentences are longer and questions more complex — 'Where Daddy gone?' and from this we move to the period of 'why' questions. At this stage it sometimes seems as if the adult never has enough knowledge to satisfy these young scientists and philosophers! I'm inclined to think of this period as the 'But why' stage rather than the 'Why' stage.

By the time the child has reached the age of three a great deal of progress has occurred in language development. Now the child can express herself using loudness and pitch. She should have a vocabulary of between 500 and 1,000 words and be capable of carrying on a simple conversation. The child may be slow and hesitant and adults must allow for this. The three-year-old's use of words may not reflect her understanding. For example, though able to count to ten fluently she may only understand the meaning of the numbers one, two and three. If you were to ask her for six blocks she might not be able to oblige — she has learned the list of numbers in much the same way as earlier she learned a nursery rhyme.

From three years on the child is refining and developing language and it becomes more like adult speech. She enjoys playing with language and should be afforded the opportunity to converse with other children and with adults. Too often language interaction can be the adult telling the child what to do, asking a question or reprimanding her. Quality language interaction between mothers and children has been studied and a particular style of talking — *Motherese* — seems to be used by those mothers who encourage language in their young children. Although called motherese it is not exclusive to mothers but can be found in any adult who converses with young children. It is characterised by the use of a high-pitched voice, short sentences with a stress on the familiar and the use of simple, concrete words. There is little use of abstract concepts.

To encourage a fluency and interest in communication and language children need to hear language spoken and used. Adults need to speak to children in a conversational way; children need to be read to; they need to hear and to take part in action rhymes, nursery rhymes and stories. With the very young child 'peek-a-boo' is the beginning of conversation, requiring and allowing for the turn-taking so important in dialogue. With stories, action rhymes and so on children extend their vocabulary, their awareness of concepts and the quality of their language experience is improved.

Adults working with young children should enjoy communicating; they must develop the skill of listening and take every opportunity to talk with children. Language and language interaction should form a fundamental part of the daily experience of young children and adults should include children, even the very young, in all the activities of the day.

PATTERN OF LANGUAGE DEVELOPMENT

3 months:	decrease in crying; smiles when spoken to; will gurgle and coo; may sustain coo for 15–20 seconds.
4 months:	Definite response to human voice — turns to seek out speaker.
5 months:	Vowel and consonant sounds present; plays with sounds.
6 months:	Cooing moves to babbling; most common utterances are '*ma;mu;da;di*'.
8 months:	Continuous repetition; intonation more distinct; sounds can signal emotion.
10 months:	Vocalisation mixed with sound-play; gurgling, blowing bubbles. Shows different adjustments to words heard.
12 months:	Sound sequences repeated, '*mamama*''. Words emerging; signs of understanding — 'show me your nose?'
18 months:	Definite repertoire of words. No concern to be understood. Understanding progressing.
24 months:	Expanding vocabulary; some two-word sentences. Increased interest in communicating.
30 months:	Very fast increase in rate of word acquisition. Many two-word sentences. Enjoys talking.

THEORIES OF LANGUAGE DEVELOPMENT

There are many theories of language development which endeavour to explain how children acquire language and learn to use it to communicate effectively. When asked, most people say that children learn by imitating adults. Children do imitate, but can this account for the way they acquire all language? Listen carefully to a three-year-old talking. What do you notice? Are they imitating what they hear? They are not. Their language is quite different. They may repeat a word or imitate an intonation but they also create original sentences, often with correct rules of grammar. Clearly imitation is insufficient to account for the rich development of language in young children although it does influence accent and the variety of vocabulary.

Another theory to explain language acquisition comes from the behaviourist perspective and emphasises the role of reinforcement. Reinforcement is anything that maintains a behaviour, praise for being good, a sweet for staying quiet, good examination results for study well done — these are all examples. This theory argues that children learn language because they are reinforced when they speak correctly. Once again one should observe children in conversation with adults to test this out. Do we always reinforce appropriate language? Not at all! A young girl says 'I wanna bikki' and we say 'You'd like a biscuit? Okay'. We *model* the appropriate language. There are times when we direct or correct a child's speech but not regularly or consistently enough to account for the veritable explosion of language in the third year of life.

A more complex explanation for language acquisition proposes that we have an innate, inborn capacity to acquire language, that we are born with a language structure called by Chomsky — the primary proponent of this theory — a Language Acquisition Device or LAD. This device (only a proposal, no neurological correlate has been found) enables children to combine words into grammatically consistent utterances and also helps them understand the speech of others at an early age.

In truth, no one theory can explain the phenomenon adequately. Most people agree that there is an innate predisposition to acquire language and that through a combination of environmental stimulation, imitation and reinforcement, the child emerges as a good communicator with language by the age of three.

Apart from how we learn language, another question that has exercised the minds of those studying language, centres around the age of acquisition. Is there a critical period for language development after which it simply will not occur? This is a very difficult issue to resolve as it would be ethically unacceptable to remove a child from all linguistic experiences for a period of time to examine this. There have been cases of children who have experienced serious neglect, been kept in isolation and not exposed to language in the way children would normally be.

EVIDENCE FROM NEGLECTED CHILDREN

- A famous case was that of Victor, the wild boy of Aveyron. He was found in the wild in the woods of Aveyron in the late 1800s when he was in his early teens. He was like an animal, 'walking' on all fours with matted hair, long nails and eating like an animal. Such children are referred to as 'feral' children in the literature. Victor was taken into care and attracted the interest of a young Dr Itard. Itard worked with Victor over a period of years and helped him develop social skills that allowed him to mix with people, eat at table and control his impulsive behaviour. However, no matter how hard Itard worked and encouraged Victor he did not acquire more than a few basic utterances. Itard saw this as a great failure on his part as a doctor but it seems that Victor may have passed the age at which he could develop the more complex structures of normal language.

- A more recent case was that of Genie — a young girl isolated at twenty months in the back room of her parents' house and tied to a potty chair. She was discovered at the age of thirteen and her case was reported in the mid 1970s. Genie's early environment, both emotional and linguistic, was severely impoverished. She was not allowed make any noise and was beaten if she did, nor was anyone allowed to talk to her. Once found she was cared for by a well-trained and dedicated team. She too acquired many social skills but only very basic language ability. She did develop a large vocabulary and showed good comprehension but her expressive speech was impaired. She never acquired the skill of fluent language and even her use of intonation to express a point was poorly developed.

Both of these cases suggest support for the idea of a sensitive period for language development. However, the early experiences of both these children was so deprived in so many areas it is difficult to judge what aspects, specifically, of early experiences are essential to language acquisition. Hearing language spoken and being rewarded for communicating in response to language do seem to be basic prerequisites for language acquisition.

Clearly for those working with young children it is essential that they understand the process and progress of language development and the critical role of the adults in the child's environment. Young babies need to hear language — not the static, one-sided language of radio or television but the interactive language of another human being where the opportunity to respond, converse and turn-take is available.

SOME COMMON PROBLEMS WITH LANGUAGE

While recognising the wide age variation in language acquisition it is necessary to keep an eye on possible problems. By observing language development, difficulties can be identified early and treatment may be more successful. Problems in language can include difficulties with general communication, comprehension, articulation, language delay, stuttering/stammering and echolalia. All young children exhibit a personal style of language but are, in the main, capable of communicating their needs. Where there is too strong a reliance on gesture to communicate, verbal language delay is likely. Some children have poor articulation and it may be very difficult to understand what they are saying. There may be a physical reason for this or a hearing problem that interferes with the child's expressive skills. In such situations the advice of a speech therapist on how best to help the child can be helpful. For some children it may be necessary to attend special therapy sessions.

Some children of two and three will stammer and this should not be too great a cause for concern. It reflects the child's attempts to express her ideas as quickly as they come to her, while not having the necessary verbal fluency. By being patient, and waiting to allow her say what she wants, you can ease the tension and relax the child. If a stammer persists professional help should be sought. *Echolalia* is an unusual language disorder and, as the name suggests, involves the child repeating the language she hears, word for word and often at a remove of some time. Where it is present to an unusual degree advice should be sought. Where language difficulties exist to a worrying degree it is advisable to have the child's language assessed by a speech therapist. This must be discussed with a child's parents and the final decision, in most cases, will rest with them. As you become more experienced in working with young children it becomes easier to pick up a difficulty and the earlier this can be done the better for the child.

For good quality, fluent speech to emerge children need to to have good language models, the opportunity to practise and the motivation and need to communicate. To encourage good language you must be a clear and exciting communicator and a careful and thoughtful listener. Opportunities for dialogue between adults and children, and children and children, should be created, and they often do need to be created. This will not yield a particularly quiet atmosphere but it is more likely to encourage good quality language interactions than an atmosphere where children are expected to be quiet.

SUMMARY

Children develop language at an extraordinary rate. They develop from an infant with no words to a three-year-old with a wide vocabulary and an emerging grasp of the rules of grammar.

Before children develop language they go through the pre-linguistic phase where communication is in terms of the cry, the coo and the babble. Even during this early stage there are opportunities for conversation and turn-taking between adults and babies. Adults often miss the child's first word! It rarely sounds like a 'real' word but is identified as the first sound used *consistently* to refer to a particular object or action.

Children's language can be considered at two levels — receptive and expressive. Early in language development children appear to understand more than they can express. Early sentence production shows many 'errors' of grammar when compared to adult language. It is interesting to note, however, that these 'errors' are common to all children and reflect an innate pattern to development.

There is no completely satisfactory explanation for the development of language. It seems to be a combination of imitation, reinforcement and predisposition. Studies of severely neglected children suggest that there is a sensitive period during which language can develop.

In working with young children adults must provide a rich and stimulating linguistic environment. This has to be well planned, particularly where children are in group care. There must be plenty of dialogue, conversation, songs, listening and reading. With young children adults must also be observant of possible problems. As with any area of development the early identification of problems is best for the child. One must always remember, however, that there can be a wide, normal variation between children in their rate of language acquisition dependent on personal and environmental factors.

EXERCISES

1. What is the difference between communication and language?

2. Write a short paragraph on the importance of 'turn-taking'.

3. What are the common categories of early words used by children? Make a list of words spoken by a two-year-old and count the different categories. (Note: spell the words as they are said.)

4. What does receptive language mean?

5. With a partner discuss how you might encourage the development of expressive language in young children.

6. Listen to a young child in conversation (three to five). Record the dialogue and comment on your record.

7. What are the three theories of language development? Select one and discuss it with a partner.

8. Why were studies of feral and neglected children so important to our understanding of language development?

9. Select a number of books that you feel would encourage appropriate language development for children of 0–1; 1–2; 2–3; 3–4 and 4–5 years of age. On what basis did you select the books?

10. Make a collection of action songs and rhymes that would encourage:

   • listening

   • turn-taking

   • vocabulary expansion.

chapter 8
social development

Humans are social beings and the baby is no exception. To anyone who has had contact with a very young infant this comes as no surprise — they smile, gurgle, reach for, react and enjoy the company of other humans. As they grow older the infant may become wary of strangers, slow to form friends and so on but the general trend is towards being sociable. Does it really matter if some children are more sociable than others? Is it a factor within the child or does it come from experience? These are the questions that have interested developmental psychologists when looking at the development of sociability.

ARE BABIES BORN WITH DIFFERENT TEMPERAMENTS?

Two American researchers, Alexander Thomas and Stella Chess, were interested in establishing whether babies are born with different temperaments. In their study, *Temperament and Development*, (the New York Longitudinal Study [NYLS]), they collected data on the behavioural development of a group of 133 children from early infancy into adult life. The study is longitudinal as the researchers gathered data on each child at different stages in their development over a long period of time. From their data they identified three distinct types of temperament in the infants. They called the different types of temperament the 'easy baby', the 'difficult baby', and the 'slow-to-warm-up baby' and found the following distribution in the population studied:

DISTRIBUTION OF TEMPERAMENT TYPES

1. The easy child (40%)	was quick to establish regular routines in infancy, generally cheerful and adapted easily.
2. The difficult child (10%)	was irregular in daily routine, slow to accept new experiences, tended to react negatively and cry a lot and showed a greater risk of adjustment problems in later life.
3. Slow-to-warm-up (15%)	child was inactive, a bit negative, and showed low key reactions to her environment.
4. Other (35%)	babies who did not fit the above categories neatly were deemed to exhibit 'no pattern'.

'Easy' babies are far less demanding than those deemed 'difficult'. They are smiley, cheerful, adaptable, friendly, rewarding. Difficult babies, on the other hand, are irritable, reject new foods, new situations, new people and fuss strenuously about their frequent complaints. They are finicky, fussy and trying.

All babies have their fussy moments or occasional periods of irritability but they are not necessarily difficult. A difficult baby is *consistently* irritable and over-reactive. These differences can cause problems in the interaction between the mother and her child in the very early stages of the relationship. For the mother who can accept a difficult child the problems will be less than for the mother who considers, for example, that the child's difficulties reflect her capacity as a mother. This brings us to an important concept in the study of child development, not only in respect of infant development but development in general, and that is the concept of *goodness of fit* . Thomas and Chess found that the development of children's behavioural problems in later life could not be predicted from a knowledge of the parents alone or for that matter, of the child alone, but rather from the goodness of fit — or lack of fit — of the characteristics of both parties and that the nature of the child's temperament at birth was a factor.

They found that difficult babies grew up well in families where parents were tolerant of their difficult behaviour, but they did not fare well with parents who fought their needs. Thomas and Chess stress how mistaken it is to assume that a child's behaviour problem must inevitably be due to unhealthy parental influences. Such a view results in a mistaken emphasis on the supposed pathogenic, or damaging, influence of the mother. The reality is that a wide variety of factors, including the temperamental nature of the child, can influence development.

Parent-child interaction is a two-way affair; what the parent does is as much affected by the child as vice versa. Some infants dislike being cuddled and will resist all attempts by the mother to provide close physical contact by struggling and crying. If a mother fails to pick up the child's dislike a lack of fit will occur and developmental problems may follow. The explanation for these problems lies in the *interaction* of mother and child and not in the characteristics of one or other partner alone.

SOCIAL DEVELOPMENT

Babies are social beings, they attract attention by their looks, their behaviour, crying, smiling and cooing. Most babies smile by six weeks and some children smile more than others. This early smile is a social smile not just to parents but to anything of interest or novel. For instance, if you put a mask on and look closely at a very young baby she will stare, reach and smile at the mask. With older children this same behaviour can cause distress as they recognise the difference between familiar and unfamiliar. You may have had experience of this at times like Hallowe'en where, despite great enthusiasm before the event, young children become quite upset and tearful when surrounded by others in masks.

STRANGER ANXIETY

By about five months most babies smile more at familiar than at strange adults. Their memory is improving and as memory develops there is a greater likelihood of stranger anxiety so that by seven or eight months babies may begin to show signs of responding differently to the familiar and unfamiliar. We call this differential response, where a child cries in the presence of a stranger, *making strange*. The level of anxiety will vary between children depending on the temperament of the child and her experiences with others. Where the care of a child is shared it is important to recognise this characteristic of social development. Recognising the normality of a child making strange and exhibiting anxiety at separation from the parent allows the caregiver to reassure parents that the behaviour is not unusual or unexpected. It also allows caregivers to facilitate slow entry, a settling-in period, into a shared care arrangement to minimise the level of stress for both child and parent. Carers need to be philosophical and understanding and try to facilitate a gradual separation to ease the stress for all. Separation anxiety, where a child is tearful and clingy at separation, may last for a couple of weeks and will be more pronounced in some children than in others. Where a child has had experience of interacting with a number of adults from birth she can form a variety of attachments and evidence of separation anxiety may be very slight. This does not reflect a weakness in the intensity of the child's relationship or attachment with her parents and may, indeed, reflect a secure and independent child.

CAN BABIES BE SPOILED?

Babies want and need people to smile at them, talk to them, hold them and play with them. But babies also need to be helped fit into adult schedules and the real social world. Here is one of the constant dilemmas facing those who work with young children and their families: the balance between the individual needs and desires of the child and the expectations of the group, society.

In the early months of life, babies cannot be spoiled. They are·too young to consciously manipulate parents — at this age they do not have the memory or cognitive skill to remember good things that happened and to ask for them again. However many times you pick up a crying baby and console her, she will not suppose that you will pick her up again, because she doesn't know what happened two minutes ago. It is hard not to assume that the baby does know that if she cries she will be picked up and at certain times it can appear as if she is even intentionally interrupting your day! With young babies this is not the case. The newborn baby demands attention now because she needs it now — not for ulterior motives. Meeting babies' demands is often trying and inconvenient for parents and carers but it is not fair to attribute selfish and manipulative intentions to the baby!

By three to four months memory is improving and by four or five months it is possible for babies to recall that the last time they cried they were picked up and at this stage you can begin to help children acquire alternative attention seeking behaviours. It is still a very young age at which to expect children to understand about waiting and, in general, a baby who is crying needs to be seen to. It may be something as simple as a wet or soiled nappy or it may be that the baby does not want to sleep and would be happier awake and in the company of others. Also it is possible that a baby gets 'overtired'. In a situation like this it is often holding and rocking with soothing words that will relax the baby and bring on sleep. From this you will see that, contrary to the view of some people that all a baby does is eat and sleep, babies need a lot of attention. It is for this reason that there should never be too many babies in the care of one adult. Even nature appears to acknowledge this fact as it is very rare for a mother to give birth to more than two infants and, indeed, where a mother has triplets or more the State may assist her with a home help in the early years.

ATTACHMENT

The formation of a child's first emotional relationship is widely regarded as one of the most important achievements of childhood. It is seen as the foundation stone for security, trust and the quality of later social relationships. The term *attachment* has traditionally been used to refer to the child's part in the relationship — as opposed to the term *bonding* which has come to be used for the parent's part. Attachment bonds refer to the powerful emotional tie that babies develop to their mother figure. An attachment has to be learned as it is based on experience with the other person.

Bonding and attachment are two closely related concepts and they have been used to suggest that there are special qualities particular to mother/child relationships, not shared between fathers and children or between children and other adults. This has also been used to give the mother a special obligation for her child's emotional well-being and has implications for the relationship between fathers and their children and non-biological parents and their foster or adopted children.

DO CHILDREN ONLY ATTACH TO MOTHERS?

Where there is no mother figure a child will attach to a mother substitute and this may well be the father. There is some evidence that a child will attach to another child if the opportunity to attach to an adult figure has been removed. After the Second World War Anna Freud and Sophie Dann studied a group of war orphans, who had been separated from their parents within the first year of life and been in various care arrangements, as a group, in refugee camps during the war. In 1945 they arrived at Bulldogs Bank in London. They had experienced varied care arrangements and, without a constant adult figure, appeared to form attachments to each other. This supports the idea that an attachment figure is important but also indicates that this need not necessarily be the mother, nor even an adult.

A break in an attachment relationship may produce, in the short term at any rate, some highly distressing, undesirable consequences. How early in infancy does separation from the mother or the permanent caretaker have an impact on children and cause them upset? It is generally accepted that children first become vulnerable to separation in the third quarter of the first year. Separation is now psychologically meaningful and can be emotionally disturbing. The distress peaks at around seven to eight months, at the end of the first year/beginning of the second year and again at two to three years. Onset of this anxiety can be relatively sudden and unexplained. The first half year of life is a period where separation is less traumatic and upset less intense. Where there is a choice of introducing another care arrangement to a child it has been suggested that it is best done at this stage. It is, for instance, always maintained that adoption placements ought to take place as early as possible. Where this is not possible careful attention to the child's needs and an awareness of the possibility of stress should yield a sensitivity that will make the experience less traumatic for all. Human beings are resilient and adaptable and the young child is no exception. It is recognising the underlying explanation for apparently unnecessary anxiety that allows us to respond appropriately and minimise the anxiety.

Although research is slight, there is some evidence that children who do not form attachments in the early years of their life, may form attachments quite late in childhood. Results of analyses of the experiences of foster children and adoptees suggests that this is possible. For attachments to form later, in children who have had a disrupted early life, careful steps must be taken in building up trust between the child and the foster or adoptive parents. It seems unlikely that such a life-sustaining relationship

137

as attachment could depend exclusively for its success on the single process of early, secure experience with one mother figure. There are many routes to attachment and a key factor is sensitivity and respect for the child on the part of the adult. Trust is the basis of secure attachments.

A mother who must leave a child in the care of others or who has to be apart from a young child for an extended period of time, in hospital for example, will not, necessarily disrupt the attachment system. It is unfortunately the case, however, that the notion of bonding and attachment has, to some extent, retained the status of a sacred doctrine — a *must* to which all mothers are supposed to conform in a particular way and at a particular time and which professional people are expected to encourage actively.

STUDIES OF BONDING AND ATTACHMENT

A most influential voice on the topic of attachment and bonding was **John Bowlby**, author of, among other books, *Childcare and the Growth of Love*. He saw the child's inclination to attach as an instinct, an unlearned pattern of behaviour, and believed that a mother has a natural maternal instinct, triggered by hormones, to love her child.

He argued strongly, from his own research on disturbed adolescents and from the research of others on children raised in institutions, that children need their natural mothers for positive emotional development. It is due to Bowlby, in no small measure, that parents can, for instance, visit and stay with their children in hospital and that institutional care for children is constantly under review. When he started writing, in the 1950s, orphanages were quite common. These institutions were often poorly staffed and inappropriate to full development of the individual. The move away from orphanages towards options like group home, fostering and adoption was speeded up by his work. However, these gains were achieved on the basis that the nuclear family, with the mother at home, was the norm. This is an ideal that is changing over the years and is less representative of the norm than it was forty years ago. We now have more lone parent families and, increasingly, fathers are remaining at home to share the care of children.

ATTACHMENT STYLES

Mary Ainsworth supports Bowlby's theory of infant attachment. She studied infant attachment by using the Strange Situation; she reasoned that if attachment is strong between baby and mother then the baby should show feelings of security in the presence of the mother and explore freely. If a stranger enters the room the baby should show fear and distress. If the baby is left alone with the stranger this should increase distress as evidenced by crying and searching for her mother. By observing babies responding to different situations she identified three different behaviour patterns to describe infant attachment:

- **Avoidant attachment:** About 20% of Ainsworth's middle-class infants showed this pattern of behaviour. It is characterised by a lack of evident distress in the presence of a stranger with no undue searching out of the mother.

- **Ambivalent attachment:** Some 15% of Ainsworth's sample exhibited this pattern. They seek proximity to the mother initially. When she leaves they seek her out but on her return they show anger and no inclination to be close to her.

- **Secure attachment:**   65% of Ainsworth's sample were securely attached. That is they behaved as Ainsworth expected — close contact to mother, distress on separation and seeking out of mother accompanied by crying until she returns. On her return the infants seek contact and their crying ceases.

The basic assumption underlying Ainsworth's work is that those infants who are securely attached are the best adapted. However, certain cultures encourage different degrees of independence in their young children. Grossman (1985) placed German infants in the Strange Situation and a higher percentage exhibited avoidant attachment than one would expect from Ainsworth's study. German parents encourage independence and would approve of this behaviour as adaptive and appropriate; Ainsworth would, however, consider it to be maladaptive. This is one of many examples of where one must be careful in interpreting results of research. It is important to know what methods are used, what sample studied and what views the researcher holds in the area of study.

In studies using the Strange Situation with young children attending daycare, a lower than expected percentage of infants exhibited 'secure' attachment behaviour. This has been interpreted to mean that daycare may be damaging to children under a year old. However, it is possible to interpret these results as indicating that these children, with their experience of a variety of carers (where care is of good quality and stable), may be more independent and no less attached to their parents than their peers raised in the home. A study by B.E. Andersson (1989) in Sweden suggests that where children are placed in good quality daycare before the age of one year they show better social skills, among other qualities, than peers who did not have this early experience.

Much of the debate on the subject of attachment centres around the idea of a mother working outside the home and how this might affect the child. The fact that a mother is employed involves a number of related issues and how it affects her children will be determined, at least in some way, by them all. They include the reason she is working; the extent to which she experiences role sharing; the father's attitude and participation in childcare; the child's temperament and the quality of substitute care.

Bowlby's assertion that the mother (or substitute mother) is crucially important in the early years and that separation from the mother figure can have long-term damaging effects has been disputed by, among others, Michael Rutter. From his research, particularly his work on the Isle of Wight study, he argued that attachment bonds can sustain separation. It is the *type* of separation that the child experiences rather than the *fact* of separation that is crucial. His arguments are well stated in his book on the topic, *Maternal Deprivation Reassessed*. Rutter also found that the quality of the attachment relationship between the child and her mother can be improved by the fact of the mother working. For example, in a situation where the mother is a lone parent the opportunity to work, while a child is cared for in a good quality service, could improve the quality of life for both the mother and the child.

The establishment of the mother's bond with her child is a highly complex, gradual and ever-changing process. To treat it otherwise merely prevents the detailed analysis that is required in understanding any interpersonal relationship. Early studies into the extent to which a mother's daily absence from home influenced her relationship with her child, focused on the damage or harm done to the young child by the mother's absence. More recent research evidence, for example that by Andersson, suggests that there may be gains for both the child and the parent where they are separated for a period each day. Rutter has suggested that there are positive effects of having more than one attachment figure for babies. Babies with more than one attachment figure are less distressed when their mother leaves. They are more content and playful in the presence of other adults which suggests that they feel secure with people other than their mothers. This is a topic that is still, however, generating a lot of research and debate.

If while caring for children of parents who work, the adult, at the same time, believes that a child should best be cared for at home by the parent, there may be a conflict. In such a situation the child may well suffer as a result of ambivalent feelings. For those working with young children, and sharing the care with parents, it is essential to recognise the complexity of this issue. For shared care to work it must have good communication between all those involved in the care of the child, stability, a clear routine and not too many carers. The implication for those working with children is clear — be sure it is a serious commitment and have confidence in your ability to provide high quality shared care to the benefit of the child and family alike.

DEVELOPING SOCIABILITY

The development of sociability refers to the making of friends and adjustment to the norms of society. It also refers to the development of skills that help this process. Observations of babies in contact with each other show that initial peer interactions are isolated and non-reciprocated and cannot be considered as real friendship. Gradually these evolve into complex, co-ordinated interaction sequences more typical of childhood. The development of sociability to peers parallels the development of important language and cognitive (reasoning) capacities. It used to be believed that babies did not interact socially with one another at all: more recent observation studies challenge this view. Social acts, such as smiling and looking, have been observed in pairs of infants by six months and by the second half of the first year smiling, laughing, touching and gesturing have been observed. It is important to be aware of this social aspect of early life as it is essential to remember that babies are social beings. Rudimentary peer sociability is present during infancy but it is also important not to exaggerate the social capacities of babies. Even where the opportunities are present for infant-to-infant socialisation, contacts are infrequent and sustained social interaction is rare.

As infants become toddlers social interactions are more sustained and with the onset of the preschool period the frequency and quality of child to child interactions change substantially. This is seen most obviously in their play, their co-operation and their ability to play harmoniously together. This aspect of social development is dealt with in more detail under the section of play.

FRIENDSHIP FORMATION

Children's ideas about friendship change as they develop. At an early age when asked about friends, children of four to seven years regard friends as those with whom one plays or shares material goods. Friendship is understood in very concrete terms. Friendship for most children is formed easily at this age, it's just a question of saying 'hi' and joining in. As easily as they are made, however, they are broken by refusing to share, hitting out or not being around to play.

During middle childhood, eight to eleven years, friendship becomes a more mutual affair. Friendship now involves not only sharing materials but includes giving help, being kind and not taking advantage of each other. Where friendships are broken at this stage they may not be easily repaired and will require apologies and explanations unlike the volatile situation of earlier friendship. By early adolescence (eleven to fifteen) friendship is understood at greater depth. The trust and loyalty elements

are important and friends are seen as those with whom you share your intimate thoughts and feelings. Because of the level of understanding, sharing and trust required at this level of friendship a serious breach in the relationship can lead to a break in the friendship.

There is remarkable agreement among researchers as to the developmental pattern of this important social area. Friendship develops in line with the child's cognitive ability — as the child gets older they can think about and understand the abstract concepts of trust, loyalty, justice . . . necessary to intimate friendship formation. The younger child cannot understand these abstract concepts and therefore has a fairly concrete and utilitarian view of friendship. The pattern of children's thinking has been discussed in an earlier section and it would be worthwhile reviewing the pattern of friendship formation in that regard. As social beings, the creation of opportunities to form friendship is important. In working with children we must provide opportunities for social interaction even with the very young. There are children who find it difficult to make friends. They may lack the social skills necessary to enter into friendships. Research suggests that through careful use of guided role play such children can, even at quite an early age, be taught the social skills. The earlier one picks up the need in children and the earlier one can help them develop appropriate skills, the better.

EMOTIONAL DEVELOPMENT

By emotions we mean the basic feelings human experience, joy, anger, happiness and so on. Emotions are usually aroused by external events and emotional reactions are directed towards these events. Defining emotions is difficult and yet working with children we frequently find ourselves talking in terms of emotions — 'she's a very happy child' or 'look at John, he's a bit sad today'. Characteristics and changes in emotional development are less visible than in physical development but no less important. We have seen from the work of Thomas and Chess that the baby has a rich emotional life from birth. She cries when hungry or left unattended and coos with content when satisfied. During the second year development is seen in the area of physical and language skills. It is also evident in her growing reasoning skills but emotions may yet be difficult to control and the child may fly into a fury or a tantrum at some very minor issue. The rage is not at the adult alone but also the activity that thwarts her. For example, the young child pulling a trolley around a room; turning, it gets caught in the leg of a chair/table; she pulls, pulls again, cries out, stamps her feet, pulls again and screams in frustration. She doesn't want help — she wants the trolley to do what she wants. Such episodes need to be handled carefully! You don't want simply to solve the problem for the child — you want to encourage better control of emotions so that the problem can be considered and a solution sought by the child.

The power of emotion: An emotion can wholly possess a child and frustration take over: control is difficult. Aspects of emotion to consider in observing children include the dimensions of mature/immature; moody/restless; content/calm; possessive/sharing. Children may be ahead in one area of development — for example you might have a four-year-old physically as tall as her peers for whom intellectual work such as letter recognition and numbers appears easy but whose emotional development, e.g. ability to express frustration in a verbal rather than a physical way, may be weak.

Fears are a further aspect of emotion. It is not easy to understand the fears of young children and apparently unrealistic fears need to be treated with respect. The power of the imagination and fantasy in the early years may fuel fears and sensitivity is needed. The fear of the dark, for instance, is a very real fear for some children and it can come on suddenly after years of sleeping in the dark. Using low lighting can help here and dimmer switches are particularly useful. The careful use of books about such topics as monsters, robbers, the dark and so on can also be very useful. I have found that when reading a sad story or one involving a monster, young children may ask you to cover over the picture or skip a few pages! Despite this they still want the story read. This is their way of allowing the fear into their lives, in a measured way, so that they can cope with it bit by bit. Where this arises one should respect the wishes of the child and not ridicule the apparent lack of logic. It is, after all, a little like those of us who go to a film and spend some of the time with our hands over our faces: despite the fear we still sit it out to the end.

Cause and effect in emotion: The child isn't always aware of cause and effect. If a child is angry and raging at an adult in a nursery and this coincidentally occurs just before the staff member takes a scheduled half-day the child may assume that her anger led to the staff member leaving. It is easy to demand adult behaviour of children — 'pull yourself together', 'don't be such a baby' or 'don't be ridiculous'. Such comments afford no support for the child who doesn't understand the powerfulness of emotions and has yet to acquire the skills of emotional control.

A child needs help when in a tantrum or a rage. Physical contact like lifting and comforting while the crying subsides is helpful. Care must be taken to avoid eye

contact, however, as this can be a very powerful reward. Give little active attention to the child until the tantrum has subsided or eased. Where a child is kicking out one must be careful not to get injured but being close by and talking calmly can help. It is of no value to get cross with the child. If you, as an adult, shout or scream it will frighten the child. When adults become unreasonably and uncontrollably angry the child is vulnerable, physically and psychologically. Following an outburst by an adult it is worth apologising to a child and explaining the situation to the child or children as far as is possible. To say 'I am sorry I shouted, I am tired and expected too much of you', is helpful as it may guide a child's understanding of emotions and emotional control. It is difficult for a child to learn self-control if the adults around her don't exhibit self-control: there is no model.

The move towards independence so evident in the two-year-old's 'No — do it self', 'I don't want to' expressions is often a source of conflict and confrontation. Knowing that this is developmentally appropriate allows us to respond constructively to such shows of independence and as the child approaches three she becomes less self-willed, more emotionally controlled and more amenable to adult direction. This is not to say that there are no tantrums but the control of emotions is improving.

Emotions are healthy: It is, of course, healthy to express different emotions. The child who exhibits very strong self-control and is never inclined to cry, rage or appear unhappy may in fact be overly controlled and this can be damaging in future development. We must be able to express our emotions in an accepted fashion.

Being unhappy means a child cares about something. If she had no concern she wouldn't feel unhappy or guilty or whatever and this would prove problematic to later social development.

We observe children in their imaginative, pretend play practising control over emotions by transferring the feeling to dolls or other toys. A young boy playing in the home corner of a nursery held a teddy by the hand and rubbed it gently. He then lay the teddy on a bed and said 'The doctor will make you better — don't be afraid'. He played on in this way tucking the teddy up, encouraging him to be brave and so on. One of the staff told me he was a twin whose brother was in hospital. His play reflected his own attempt to understand his emotions of fear, unhappiness and loneliness.

There are a variety of ways to express emotions and these include: smiling/laughing when happy; withdrawing when frightened; crying when frustrated and being aggressive when angry or frustrated.

A WORD ABOUT AGGRESSION

Aggression is an emotion that causes concern to those with children. Most people experience aggressive thoughts and impulses at some time. How we handle these thoughts and impulses will have a major effect on our personal health and on our inter-personal relations. There is evidence that aspects of aggression are learned and the social learning theory argues that aggressive responses can be learned through imitation and increased if positively reinforced. Evidence suggests that experiencing aggressive behaviour can either increase subsequent aggressive behaviour or maintain it at the same level.

When a four-year-old hits her two-year-old brother in an emotional outburst, how the adult responds is important. If the adult slaps the child and says 'Never let me see you hit your brother' the adult is delivering a mixed message to the child. The adult is saying 'I'm in charge and I'll hit you to make you behave so that you don't hit your brother'. The adult is modelling the very behaviour she wants the child to stop and yet it is likely that she will be imitated and so is, in fact, strengthening the behaviour.

Indirect, observed or *vicarious* expressions of aggression may also increase or maintain aggressive behaviour in children. There seems to be a positive relation between the amount of exposure children have to, for example, televised violence and expressions of violence in their behaviour, even where this is cartoon violence. Studies also show sex differences with girls tending to imitate aggressive behaviour much less than boys do unless specifically rewarded for doing so.

Does viewing violence lead to an increase in aggressive behaviour?

It appears to and the following are some possible explanations for the mechanism of influence:

TV factors and aggression	
1. Modelling aggressive styles of conduct	Children imitating what they see.
2. Increasing arousal	Watching violent rather than non-violent television programmes can lead to emotional arousal which may spill over into aggressive behaviour if a child is frustrated/angry.
3. Desensitising people and violence	Continual exposure to television violence blunts emotional expression. It may affect our ability to empathise and allows us to accept higher levels of aggressive behaviour.
4. Reducing restraints on aggressive behaviour	Generally there are social constraints which minimise or decrease the likelihood of our injuring or hurting others. Observing others behaving aggressively, however, may weaken these restraints.
5. Distorting views about conflict resolution	Aggressive action to resolve interpersonal conflicts is more common on TV than using other methods, such as verbal reasoning. This is understandable given the value of visual impact. It may distract, however, the sense of how conflict should be resolved and may lead young children to consider violence as an acceptable form of conflict resolution — reflecting their difficulty in keeping fiction/fantasy and reality separate.

Research suggests that viewing aggression affects social behaviour differently in different children. Why should this be so? It appears that children who are having school/social problems, or who identify more with violent characters, are more likely to be affected by television violence. Social factors which seem associated with anger and aggression in young children include poverty, overcrowding, a sense of loss of control, low self-esteem.

TV viewing is not all bad. It affords a good opportunity for relaxation, it can be enjoyable and it can be informative. With young children, who are not yet discriminating in their viewing, TV should be watched with an adult at least part of the time. This will allow children to ask questions or prompt adults to make a particular point. It may also allow adults to distract children if material that is considered unsuitable is showing. If adults model appropriate use of the TV as a source of information and enjoyment the young child will pick up on this. For example, it is good practice to look up the TV guide and select a programme or two to watch; watch only these programmes and turn the TV off when they are finished. This helps children realise that the TV is like a game or a book and can be returned to as necessary. Using the TV as a 'babysitter' is not good practice and there is still debate as to how daycare services should use TV.

Emotions are individual and complex. People have different levels of emotional expression: these may be aggravated or controlled by environmental factors. In working with young children we must try to understand their emotional development in terms of the factors in their lives rather than evaluate it against some measure that reflects our own experiences and expectations alone.

PERSONALITY DEVELOPMENT

In any discussion about the development of personality the views of **Sigmund Freud** (1856–1939) must be considered. Here was a man, writing at the turn of the twentieth century whose theories cannot be easily tested but whose influence is still far-reaching. A major contribution to thinking in the area of development — and particularly child development — was his view of the unconscious, that part of the human mind that is not immediately accessible to us. Freud identified the unconscious as a convenient metaphor for material not in our awareness but which influences our daily emotions and actions. He argued that many 'slips of the tongue' allowed us insight into the unconscious factors directing our behaviour. He also argued that certain characteristics in individuals such as a tendency to lose things, rigorous punctuality, greed and miserliness could be explained. They are not accidents — they have meaning.

Freud saw the individual personality being shaped by experiences and interpretations of experiences from very early in life. Indeed he considered the first seven years of life as crucial. From his research — carried out primarily with adult female patients and influenced very much by the period in which he lived — he proposed the existence of a sexual energy, the libido, in each of us. This libido, he argued, acted as a life force and was essential to reproduction and the survival of the species. Here we can pick up, perhaps, the influence of Darwin and the 'origin of the species'. The libido finds expression in different parts of the body at different stages in development. How this is responded to by the individual and significant people in her life directs the development of her personality. The libido is not something tangible, observable or visible: it is merely a proposal that Freud made to account for aspects of his theory of personality development.

There are, he proposed, three portions of the individual personality, the *id*, *ego* and *superego*, which become integrated and balanced over time during a sequence of five stages. By id Freud meant the inherited desires seeking immediate satisfaction which are present in us all at birth. The ego emerges in early infancy to assist in the satisfaction of the id impulses in accordance with reality. Using the growing power of reason and memory the child learns to delay her demands until the appropriate time. The superego develops towards the end of early childhood, around seven or eight. The superego emerges as the conscience of the individual. This is the influence of societal values and it rules over the ego and id. The superego develops from the child's interactions with parents and significant others.

FREUD'S STAGES OF PERSONALITY DEVELOPMENT

Freud identified five stages in the development of the person towards the balance between the id, ego and superego. At each stage the sexual impulses, directed by the libido, shift their location of expression. Freud believed that the experiences and conflicts during these stages, and how conflicts were resolved, directed the way personality developed and could account for different traits in individuals. This is a theory that is almost impossible to prove but despite this it has had a profound influence on clinical practice over the years.

The five stages Freud proposed were:

•   Oral stage (first year)

•   Anal stage (1–3 years)

•   Phallic stage (3–6 years)

- Latency period (6–puberty)

- Genital stage (puberty onwards)

The Oral Stage: at this period the id seeks pleasure and satisfaction through the oral (mouth) region of the body. The emerging ego directs the sucking activities of the baby towards the bottle or breast to satisfy hunger. Where oral needs are not satisfied, Freud argues, the unfulfilled person is likely to develop habits such as nail-biting, thumb-sucking or pencil-chewing in childhood and over-eating or smoking at a later stage.

The Anal Stage: during the Anal Stage pleasure is derived from the anal areas of the body and can be associated with toileting and toilet training. Here the ego must learn to postpone pleasurable release until the appropriate time and place. This is a period where conflict can arise between parents and child. Where parents are too strict or insistent on success the conflicts may lead to later behaviours such as orderliness, cleanliness or, indeed, disorder and messiness.

The phallic stage: the focus for the id impulses has moved to the genital area. It is during this period that Freud proposed the occurrence of the Oedipus complex: this refers to the stage where a young boy so loves his mother that he wishes for his father's death. He is, however, overcome by the fear of punishment by his father and, in order to retain the parent he loves he takes on the characteristics of his father, his values and attitudes. This is called *identification* and recognised as an important process in development. While it is very difficult to prove its existence Freud argued that it is through such conflicts that a child learns the social norms, through his identification with the adult role model. A similar Electra complex is proposed for girls. It is by resolving these conflicts, Freud argues, that the superego begins to form and the relationship between the three dimensions of id, ego and superego becomes established.

The latency period follows where, Freud proposed, the sexual instincts lie dormant. The child enjoys activity and adventure and identifies with the same sex peers and takes on, more clearly, the values of her surrounding culture.

The genital stage: finally, after puberty, the individual reaches the period of sexual maturity. If previous development has been healthy Freud concludes that the individual will follow the natural path of marriage, mature sexual relations and the birth and rearing of children.

Freud's theory is important because it was the first to identify early experiences as important to later development and it highlighted the important influence of relationships, particularly within families, to later development. However, it is increasingly criticised as having overemphasised the sexual motivation for behaviour and failing to recognise that the developmental experiences of a social and intellectual nature also prepare one for the future. Also, the theory is weak as it derives from work with repressed, middle-class adults in a culture and time far removed from our own and Freud never studied children directly.

Eric Erikson (1902–) expanded Freud's stages to include development across what he called the Life Span. He presented a broader view and he de-emphasised the prominent role of sexuality. He emphasised the psycho*social* aspects of development where Freud focused on the psycho*sexual*. He also considered that important developmental experiences occur at all stages of life and not just the early years as Freud proposed.

In the stages suggested — the first five of which parallel Freud's stages — Erikson identifies a series of conflicts which present at each stage. How those conflicts are resolved, positively or negatively, will direct the course of development for each individual.

COMPARING FREUD'S AND ERIKSON'S STAGES

Period of development	Freud's psychosexual stages	Erikson's psychosocial stages
Birth–1 year	Oral Stage	Basic Trust v Mistrust
1–3 years	Anal Stage	Autonomy v Shame & Doubt
3–6 years	Phallic Stage	Initiative v Guilt
6 years–puberty	Latency Period	Industry v Inferiority
Puberty & Adolescence	Genital Stage	Identity v Role Diffusion
Young Adulthood		Intimacy v Isolation
Middle Adulthood		Generativity v Stagnation
Old Age		Ego Integrity v Despair

Basic Trust v Mistrust: during this first stage, the development of trust in others depends on a warm and secure early environment. Where infants have to wait too long for comfort or attention or where they are handled hastily or inconsistently, a mistrust will develop.

Autonomy v Shame and Doubt is the second stage proposed by Erikson. Autonomy is achieved where parents and others foster the development of the child in a way that is appropriate to her developmental stage. Where adults are over-strict or restricting they may shame the child leading to a sense of doubt rather than autonomy.

Initiative v Guilt: during this period children begin to take on roles and develop a sense of independence and self-control. Adults assist this by providing opportunities for increased independence. Difficulties can arise where adults make unrealistic demands for self-control in children and this can yield feelings of guilt in the child. The fourth stage proposed by Erikson is that of **Industry v Inferiority**. This is a period where children are in formal education, have the opportunity for co-operative experiences and friendship formation. The feeling of failure that can arise through school failure or poor social experiences may yield a sense of inferiority.

Identity v Role Diffusion refers to that period of transition from childhood to adulthood. Erikson believed that this is the period where past experiences, both positive and negative, direct the individual towards a sense of identity. When adolescents are confused about their role and where they are going in life they may suffer what is called role diffusion. Young adulthood is marked by a move to the period of **Intimacy v Isolation:** having developed a personal identity one moves towards more intimate relations, including close friendships. When difficulties arise at this stage in the formation of such relationships one can feel a sense of isolation.

The move towards middle age sees a move to **Generativity v Stagnation**. This stage refers to the positive task of encouraging the future generation through, for instance, childrearing and caring for others. Where no opportunity for this arises one can experience a sense of failure and stagnation. The final stage proposed by Erikson is of **Ego Integrity v Despair** and refers to old age. This is a time for looking back and evaluating life. Where life appears worth living one experiences integrity; however, when the review presents a life perceived as a failure a sense of despair will be experienced.

Currently psychoanalytic theory does not occupy an influential position in child development studies. It is descriptive, based on values and beliefs of an era long past and the conclusions derived are difficult to test and virtually impossible to prove or disprove. Nonetheless, the work of Freud and Erikson and others provided an important stimulus to developmental research and focused attention on issues of current importance such as attachment, aggression, childrearing practices, moral development and adolescent identity.

CHILDREARING

Childrearing influences the later behaviour of children as well as that immediately observed. Methods of childrearing vary from country to country and, indeed, from one time to another. In the early part of the twentieth century childrearing practices were fairly strict, parents were advised not to spoil their children by picking them up every time they cried. Toilet training was to occur in the first year, thumb sucking was to be discouraged, 'bad' habits to be replaced by 'good' ones. Little children needed to be socialised — firm control was the order of the day.

The middle of the century saw a switch towards more permissive and flexible childrearing. Parents were advised to follow their inclinations, adopt flexibility of style to fit in with the pattern of the child, while at the same time helping them adapt to your patterns. For instance, improved understanding of physical and psychological development led to the recommendation that toilet training should only begin when the child was physically mature and old enough to understand the process, certainly not before eighteen months. It is always hard to recognise a trend when living through it, but there is some evidence of a move in childrearing practice away from extreme permissiveness, towards a *balanced* approach with moderate control and firm discipline. Children have flourished under the various methods of childcare and this is surely a tribute to their adaptability! Specific practice is probably less important than a basic attitude of love, care and respect from parents and carers.

Parents' reports of how they handle their children and the type of childrearing methods they use are not always very reliable. Parents tend to report what they think they should do rather than what they actually do. This makes it difficult to predict how different practices affect different behaviours. Although it is difficult to link specific childrearing practice to later characteristics, we do know something about what constitutes a good style of childcare as opposed to a poor type.

WHICH PARENTING STYLE?

Studies suggest that parents who are firm and consistent in the expectations of how children should behave and who are also warm and affectionate and respect their children's opinions tend to produce competent and self-reliant preschoolers. Parents who are very controlling and more concerned with their own needs than those of their children, tend to produce offspring who may be self-controlled, but not very secure or confident in new situations or when meeting new people; and parents who are permissive, who do not establish clear limits and are inconsistent in their handling of behaviour — not rewarding appropriate behaviour or discouraging inappropriate behaviour — produce children who are low on self-control and self-reliance.

The first parent type has been labelled the democratic or authoritative parent and children experiencing such practice are active, outgoing, friendly, independent, creative and disobedient. The controlling parent may be considered dominant or authoritarian expecting children to 'do so because I say so'. Here children may internalise anger, may behave appropriately through fear rather than understanding and have an increased likelihood of suffering anxiety and depression-related problems later in life. Finally the permissive and inconsistent parent may have children who are indifferent, delinquent or not self-assured. The value in recognising these trends for those working with children is that understanding your own experiences can explain your own behaviour and knowing what is most beneficial to children allows you to try and behave in this way.

The following dimensions of childrearing have been identified as a means of explaining how different early experiences can yield different outcomes. Taking the dimensions of Autonomy (Freedom) v Control and Love v Hostility the different combinations that emerge can be seen below.

Dimensions in childrearing*

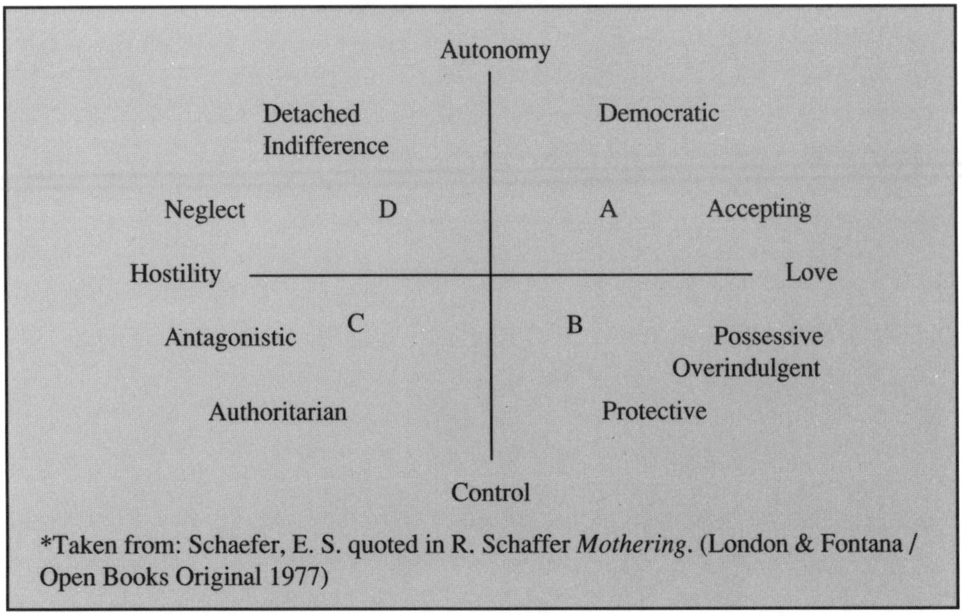

*Taken from: Schaefer, E. S. quoted in R. Schaffer *Mothering*. (London & Fontana / Open Books Original 1977)

A. A child experiencing this type of parenting shows the characteristics typical of democratic parenting; she is likely to be active, outgoing, friendly, independent, creative and disobedient.

B. A child from this background will tend to be neat, polite, dependent and conforming.

C. This background may produce a child who internalises anger and there is an increased likelihood of neuroses.

D. A child experiencing this type of parenting may act out resentment with an increased tendency to delinquency.

One must remember that the situations outlined above are a simple representation of the possibilities. The reality is often more complex. For instance in a two parent family one might have a father typical of quadrant C and a mother typical of quadrant A. Their parenting styles will interact to some degree and the outcome here is more difficult to predict. Use the above as a broad guide — not as a statement of absolute fact.

SUMMARY

Humans are social beings and, it appears from studies such as that by Thomas and Chess, that babies are born with temperamental characteristics that affect the quality of social interaction.

A key development in the early years is the formation of an attachment bond — an emotional tie between a child and another. In general this 'other' is the parent or parent substitute but in certain, rare, instances it has been found that children will attach to other children.

John Bowlby proposed that the positive attachment bond between an infant and her mother was instinctive and crucial for future mental health. His influence was immense and many of the positive developments in the field of childcare are due to him. However, his belief in the crucial importance of the mother and the damage of separation appears to have been overstated. Work by many authors, among them Michael Rutter, suggests that, while it is important for a child to form attachment bonds, this need not be with the mother or mother figure. Furthermore, the experience of separation may not be damaging — it is the cause and type of separation that seems to influence the outcome.

Working with young children to provide high quality care requires a ratio of adults to children that will allow children to form attachment bonds with their carers as well as their parents. Careful planning for settling in new children and good lines of communication between parents and carers facilitates this process.

Friendship formation has a developmental pattern which reflects the child's cognitive development. Before intimate, trusting friendships can be formed children must understand the abstract concepts of, say, trust and loyalty. In young children this is not possible and friendships can be formed for quite utilitarian reasons: 'I like her because she lets me ride her bike', and may not last for very long.

Emotions are our basic human feelings. They are influenced by our own predisposition and our experiences. Many emotional characteristics are acquired. Children may need help in learning how to understand and control their emotions.

Freud and Erikson have contributed to our understanding of personality development. Their theories of psychosexual and psychosocial stages (respectively) have provided an interesting, if somewhat controversial, model from which to view personality characteristics. Their work has focused attention on the importance of childrearing practices, early experiences and the resolution of conflict to the development of a healthy personality.

Childrearing practices have been found to influence children's development. The 'democratic' style is acknowledged as the model most likely to produce well-adjusted children: the more 'authoritarian' style is associated with later maladaptive behaviour.

EXERCISES

1. Describe the study carried out by Thomas and Chess. Outline the different types of temperament found in young babies.

2. What is meant by an 'attachment bond' and 'goodness of fit' ?

3. With a partner discuss what you know about the work of John Bowlby. How has he influenced childcare practice? Share your findings with another pair of students.

4. Do babies need mothers? Support your answer by reference to research.

5. What is meant by 'maternal deprivation'? What was Michael Rutter's contribution to the debate about maternal deprivation?

6. How can you assist children in settling into a shared care arrangement? Identify three practical ways this could be done.

7. How does your understanding of the pattern of friendship formation influence your work with three to five-year-olds? Discuss this with a partner.

8. Observe — on a practical placement, if possible — the way an aggressive episode is handled. Discuss your observations with a group in the light of what you know about child development and emotional control. Would you have handled it any differently? If so — in what way and why?

9. Compare Freud's and Erikson's approach to describing the stages of personality development. Write a short essay to highlight the similarities and differences.

10. How does your knowledge of personality development influence your practice with young children?

11. List the characteristics of parenting styles outlined in this chapter. Which style is considered best? Why?

chapter 9
encouraging
good behaviour

In the previous chapters we have discussed the normal development of the young child. There are, of course, problems that can be encountered in the behaviour of children and many of these are quite normal also. In this chapter I will outline some of the more common problems you are likely to be faced with when working with young children.

In any setting where there are a number of children of different ages it will be necessary to discourage behaviour which leads to disharmony and distress and to encourage good behaviour. There are a number of principles that facilitate the maintenance of harmony. To begin with the adult must create a positive environment and develop positive tactics to manage behaviour rather than resorting to more negative controlling techniques. Instead of saying 'don't do that' say instead 'Try to do this'. You need to find a balance so that the praise for good and appropriate behaviour to any one child at least equals the negative attention she gets. Observational studies of adult-child interactions, particularly in school settings, have found that some children only receive negative attention!

It is also important to give positive feedback to children on their behaviour. This is most effective when it closely follows the particular behaviour. Have simple rules and alert a child immediately she shows signs of doing something unacceptable. Where a child's own actions lead to immediately experienced and understood consequences it is most likely to have a positive effect.

In creating an atmosphere or environment that encourages appropriate behaviour the physical environment needs to be considered, Too much furniture and equipment creates a greater likelihood of children bumping into each other which can, in turn, increase the incidence of aggressive physical contact. Ensuring that there are good pathways for movement where there are young children should decrease the incidence of such behaviour.

Children are individuals with different interests, temperaments and coping skills. In your daily contact with groups of young children you are likely to come across a wide variety of difficult or problem behaviours that will vary from the simple to the more complex. In line with the general view of this book it is important to remember that children behave in response to their experiences. They are not always able to tell us how they feel or express why they are behaving in a particular way. For this reason it is necessary to try and understand a child's behaviour, what is causing her to behave in a particular way at a particular time and to try to meet her needs while at the same time changing her behaviour so that it becomes more acceptable. This can be done by equipping her with new skills, for instance, encouraging her to use words rather than cry when frustrated.

SOME COMMON PROBLEMS

The types of problems that arise will vary depending on the age and ability of the children with whom you work. They tend to centre around similar issues however. Problems that are commonplace and arise early in any contact with children can be associated with *separation*. You will recall that children from seven or eight months are inclined to make strange and cry if left in the company of unfamiliar adults. This is developmentally appropriate behaviour. However, this type of behaviour can also occur with older children when they are separating from parents. This can show itself in tears and clingy behaviour or in the child becoming very withdrawn. Withdrawal as an expression of anxiety must be looked out for carefully as it is much less noticeable than the behaviour of the child that cries or disrupts. Separation will affect children differently at different ages and they will express their feelings in different ways. Where the care of a child is shared all the adults involved should prepare the child carefully. Parents should take time to introduce the child to the new situation and the new adults. If the child will be attending a nursery or the home of a minder she should be brought for short visits to settle in before attending regularly. There should be good communication between the parents and the carer so that the child, even the very young child, senses trust between them and can come to trust the unfamiliar adult. It is, for instance, important that parents can come right into the house or room where the child will spend most of her time. Older children like to show parents around and it will help younger children experience continuity of care.

Many people advocate a slow settling-in period to help overcome the stress associated with separation and, where practicable, this is a very good idea. Settling-in means having the child and parent come together and stay for a short time, come again and stay a little longer. As this happens the child will become more relaxed and comfortable. When the time is right, and it will differ from child to child, the parent can leave for a short time. It is important that the parent says goodbye to the child and makes it clear that she/he will return shortly. Having said a clear goodbye it is important for the parent to leave immediately as a delay can make the leavetaking more complicated than necessary. Sneaking away when the child is occupied and not looking is not to be encouraged — it can cause more trauma: it breaks any trust that has developed and is more difficult to overcome in the long run.

OVERDEPENDENCE

There are some children who are very dependent on their parents and we call them overdependent. Overdependence can be seen in even very young children and it has many causes. Where a child is unnecessarily dependent, and this is a conclusion that only can be drawn by careful observation and discussion with parents, some firmness at separation by all parties is necessary. To begin with, the child must be told what is happening; 'protecting' a child by not telling her the plans until the last minute will only lead to distrust. The child may be allowed to keep something from home or belonging to the parent during the day and this may act as a contact point for the child.

Once confident that the child is happy in the new environment the parent should leave for short breaks, even where the child shows signs of upset. Many a parent has left with a child crying and stood outside the door only to hear sounds of joy after a few short minutes. However, where a child is clearly distressed and not settling it may be wiser to consider putting off the separation for a short time. With experience, it is usually easy to identify this type of dependent behaviour.

The other form of separation difficulty that can arise is where the parent does not feel comfortable about leaving. This can be seen in the parent who says goodbye, moves away, comes back again to say goodbye and so on. This can be very stressful for the child and, where initially she accepted the leaving, she may now become upset. Parents who fall into this category need gentle but firm handling.

In general one should try to make separation as easy as possible. There needs to be clear messages of trust between the adults, a spare lap or arms for the new child, the opportunity for a settling-in period with the parents and freedom for the child to just settle at her own pace. The old notion that a short, sharp separation was best for all concerned is now recognised as inappropriate. It does not allow the child time to adjust and actively cope with the changing situation, rather it encourages a passive acceptance and forces the child to adapt too quickly. This can compromise the quality of the experience from the very beginning.

TEMPER TANTRUMS

Temper tantrums are another common behaviour in young children. They often reflect the child's frustration at her own inability to solve problems or to make a point clearly in a way that will be understood. They are normal in toddlers but become a problem if handled incorrectly by, for instance, giving in to the child too easily. In this case the child manipulates the situation and is controlling the adult by resorting to a tantrum if not getting her own way. Firm and immediate handling in a warm and accepting way generally lessens the intensity of the tantrum and also leads to a decrease in incidence.

Where limits and rules are simple, few and clear to the child, the likelihood of confusion and frustration is less. If you are shopping and a child wants sweets at the checkout, it is more likely to be resolved quietly if you have already indicated that you will not be buying sweets and why. This can be reinforced by writing a list of what you will buy and pointing this out to the child. Using the list at the shop further reinforces the point that you will only buy what is on the list and will not be buying sweets. Given this clear information the child is less likely to have a tantrum. If, on the other hand, you simply rush around the shop without including the child in the act and say no to every request, the final request for sweets is likely to end in tears when you say no! Where a child does have a tantrum it is important to hold your ground. If you have said no, then you must try and stick to this decision. Giving in 'for a quiet life' means that you are sending the child an inappropriate message — cry and you will get what you want. It may solve the immediate problem but it is setting the scene for further difficulty ahead. It is not helping the child cope with the problem and is not assisting the development of self-control.

Only in cases where she is a danger to herself or others should a child be physically restrained during a tantrum. This is best done by holding the child from behind and using soothing words in a calm, low voice. Eye contact should be avoided as it acts as a very strong reward and may, actually, maintain the unwanted behaviour. Once calmed the child should be helped to understand — at her own ability level — why her behaviour is unacceptable and how she might cope with a similar situation again. Where the child is pulling a toy and it jams, for example, she tugs and pulls but cannot release it. A tantrum may follow. Once calmed she should be shown what the problem is and how it could be solved. A very young child will need to practise the solution a number of times but in this way you are substituting more acceptable behaviour and helping the child develop coping skills herself. It is of little value to the child in the long run simply to solve the problem for her, she must be included in the solution.

A behaviour sometimes accompanying a temper tantrum is *breath holding*. Some children learn to hold their breath during a tantrum, or as a separate behaviour. They can hold their breath until their faces turn blue. This can be a very frightening experience for the adult but, it appears, a child will faint before she does any harm to herself and, in the faint will resume breathing. Where it occurs it is best to remain calm and not force the child to breathe. When she starts to breathe again she will need comfort rather than criticism. If breath holding continues, it may be necessary to seek other professional help.

AGGRESSION

Aggression is another behaviour that causes concern to those working with young children. It can take many forms. Where a child is physically aggressive to other children or to adults every effort must be made to stop the behaviour and try to understand why it is occurring. To assess this it may be important to observe the child. Is there a particular situation in which the aggression is more likely to occur? Is there a particular child always present or at the receiving end? By observing what preceded an aggressive outburst we can sometimes intervene to redirect the child towards a more appropriate activity. One behaviour that causes real concern is *biting*. There is no quick answer to eliminating biting. In this situation both the victim and the biter need attention. The victim will need to be soothed and seen to in terms of first aid and the biter will also need to be soothed. It is of little value to ask her to 'Say you are sorry' because this is something that is meaningless unless it comes from within. A child who bites does need to find other ways of expressing anger or frustration through words or by hitting out at or biting on inanimate objects. Biting is never solved by biting back! It may stop the behaviour but it does not help the child cope with the feelings that led to the behaviour and these feelings may find expression in another inappropriate behaviour. Young children who are teething may bite.

Aggressive behaviour can also be directed at inanimate objects or the tearing of books. If a child is inclined towards this type of destructive behaviour it may be possible to redirect the energy into woodwork, football or clay modelling. All these activities, in their different ways, allow for the release of pent-up energy and emotion and are more acceptable.

Children can be aggressive for different reasons. Perhaps the child is jealous of another child and cannot express or even understand this emotion. Aggression may indicate that a child is under personal strain or is unhappy. On the rare occasions that one meets a child whose aggression runs deeper, professional help is necessary. Whatever causes a child to behave in this way we must try and understand, help her overcome the emotions leading to aggression, allow her boundaries within which to be aggressive, while at the same time setting limits. Where a child has a tendency towards aggression it might be helpful to try and 'second guess' her and distract her towards other activities. Do not be afraid to be kind and understanding. This is not being 'soft', it is being human and respectful. Criticising, ridiculing or harshly punishing a child is likely to have a long-term effect that is negative rather than positive. It is of little value to the child and not a great deal of value to the adult.

ISOLATED AND WITHDRAWN

Children who are *isolated* and *withdrawn* can also present as a problem. They may not mix socially or speak to other children or adults. Children such as this can go unnoticed for a time. When you do come across it you must try and create non-threatening opportunities for social contact between the child and adults but also between the child and other children. Using soothing activities such as water play can ease a child's shyness. It is often beneficial to pair the withdrawn child with a socially mature and kind child for activities that require co-operation and conversation.

Where children appear *bored* we must try to excite them; produce new material, suggest a change in routine, read a new story or start a different activity. Maybe they have a reason to be bored! Are the materials and books always the same? Is there a tight routine that does not allow for spontaneity? Are activities too difficult? Are they too easy? It may be convenient to know that Katie loves a particular puzzle but if she has used it to its limits it is not of much value. Are the activities too adult-led? Sometimes when we prepare an activity we can put in a lot of effort — cut out shapes, tear up paper, cut up material and have everything just right. While planning is necessary, too much planning leaves little for the child to do. If all a child has to do, for instance, is stick cotton wool on a snowman shape she can feel little ownership of the activity. We have seen that children learn best by active involvement in activities. In our planning we must ensure that we allow them the opportunity to be truly active and to have a sense of achievement and ownership. Novelty is a great force for change. Either bring out new equipment, alter the routine a little or introduce a new activity.

Some children, particularly those from inhibiting or restricting backgrounds, may have limited play skills and so *appear* to bore easily. In fact they lack the skills to play and to extend the use of materials. Here we can intervene to help the child by modelling play behaviour, we can provide opportunities for imaginative play. Dressing up and the home corner can offer a new and exciting outlet for expression. Knowing what to expect in general and knowing your children in particular can guide you in your handling of this situation.

CHILDHOOD FEARS

Almost all children show some fears during the early years. The fear of the dark is one we have mentioned earlier and is quite common and, as with all fears, it should be handled carefully. No one will overcome a fear by being told to 'grow up'. Other common fears include fear of loss, of monsters, of robbers and of death. It is wise to let children discuss death in the safety of your secure environment. You may be surprised at what it is they worry about: it could be as mundane as the dark or the cold of the ground! There is no value in hiding the reality of death and the topic should be treated seriously if it arises. There are many useful books dealing with the fears and worries of young children and they can be a valuable source of guidance in handling particular children.

SWEARING

Swearing is a problem that affects adults in different ways — most adults find it inappropriate. Tact is, however, necessary. Some children use swear words as part of their everyday vocabulary because they are part of the language they hear at home or in their neighbourhood. Others may use swear words for the shock value and here it really is best to ignore them. You can have clear rules about swear words such as 'that is not a word we use here'. Children should not be told it is bold to use such words as this could be problematic in families where they are in common usage.

SELF-HELP

With younger children problems may arise around the areas of *sleeping, feeding* and *toileting*. Most often the problems centre around a lack in pattern or predictability in sleeping, or fussiness about food. Any attempts to resolve these problems must include parents and all the adults involved need to develop a consistent and common approach. It can happen that a child exhibits a problem in the nursery that she does not show anywhere else. In this case a close look at the routine, expectations and consequences for the behaviour must be studied. With young children in particular a diary or note system between the carers and parents is a valuable source of contact. While it may be difficult to initiate, the benefits to all are immense. As a parent of a young baby in a nursery I found it helpful to have some idea of what she had eaten, how long she had slept and whether or not she had a soiled nappy. These little pieces of information can make a big difference to the smooth running of shared care.

Where older children are wetting or soiling the particular situation must be looked into. The occasional 'accident' with a three-year-old is probably no cause for concern but where a previously 'dry' child begins to wet regularly there may be some factor that has changed and is causing her upset. This should be discussed with her parents. The case of soiling is different. If an older child is soiling, or seriously constipated, her parents and herself may need to receive professional help and advice. It may be a physical problem such as an anal lesion or it may be something more complex.

THE 'BOLD' CHILD

A word about *boldness*. It is my belief that children are good. Where 'bold' behaviour is identified I believe it can be explained under a number of the points I have raised in this chapter. As adults we are in control. Our control is to be used to encourage the children in our care to develop their own self-control. If we make unrealistic demands of children they will not be able to live up to them. If we find them 'misbehaving' we owe it to them to look to ourselves and the routine first. The use of punishment procedures such as the bold chair and time out are of little value in the everyday routine. You will notice, if you use these methods, that it is often the same child sitting in the chair or going out of the room. The method is failing and you must look more closely at the causes of the behaviour. The bold chair, or the corner and such like, is a form of ridicule. It is picking out the child for negative attention and it does not help the child resolve the problem. If you find yourself saying 'I have told you before not to . . .' again and again to the same child perhaps you have not been clear in stating what exactly you do want. Removing a child from the room or an activity is an avoiding mechanism. It simply removes the child from whatever is causing the unwanted behaviour but it is not helping her to cope with the situation or learn how to alter her behaviour to make it more acceptable. There are times when things can get very fraught and a child can become particularly irritating. At certain times we all resort to procedures that do more for us, the adult, than the child. I simply caution against the use of methods that ridicule or show disrespect for the child and those that do not help the child in any way to overcome the difficulty and take control of herself.

We often expect a great deal of children. We expect them to understand the rules even where we may not have made them clear; we expect them to tell the truth although their understanding of what is true, what is fantasy and what is a lie is not at all well developed; we get cross when they are clumsy and may restrict them in what they can do because we want to avoid a mess; we get cross if they 'tell tales' and yet their intention may simply be to check out that what they thought was wrong is in fact wrong. Telling you that Sarah threw the sand may be a way of checking that it is not allowed to throw sand rather than a determined attempt to get Sarah into trouble. As

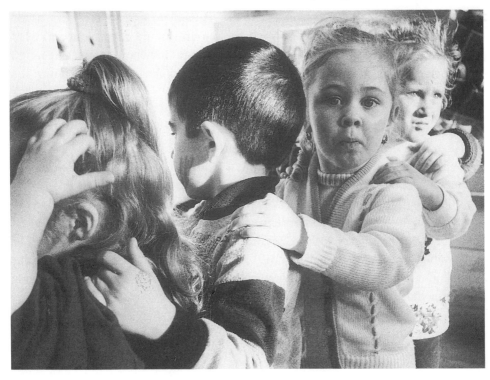

adults we must work at praising children when they behave as we would wish. Often we forget to praise good behaviour because it is no more than we would expect. We must make our wishes clear to children and to do this we must know why we want children to behave in certain ways. Maybe some of our rules reflect thoughtless habit rather than well-reasoned good practice. When children behave in unacceptable ways we must point this out clearly and try to equip them with skills that will allow them to overcome the problem themselves.

WHEN OUTSIDE HELP IS NEEDED

At some stage we may all come up against a situation that is more than simply a common problem. Behaviour that is inappropriate for age or that is severe, damaging or persistently causing concern, needs to be taken seriously. When it arises it must be handled with care and through discussion with other staff members, where appropriate, and with the parents. Some percentage of children show serious psychological or linguistic difficulties. The earlier these children can be identified and assessed and receive the appropriate support, the better for everyone. In the case of language difficulties early speech therapy may make a child's transition into primary school a success whereas a delay in treatment could mean an experience of failure in formal education. One area that is particularly difficult to deal with is suspected child abuse. There are now clear guidelines issued by the Department of Health as to what behaviours should cause concern, what procedures you should follow if you suspect abuse and how best to handle it for all concerned. Copies of the booklet *Child Abuse Checklist* are available from the Department of Health Childcare Section.

There is generally a reason behind a child's inappropriate behaviour and an explanation should be sought along with efforts to change the behaviour. It is through children's behaviour that we come to understand them and this behaviour includes their 'misbehaviour'; indeed this type of behaviour often affords a very useful insight into the child's world and how she is perceiving it. We must harness our tendency to reprimand and criticise children and work at praising their good behaviour. We should try to look beyond unacceptable behaviour and, with our understanding of development, try to find an explanation.We must look at our expectations and our practice and try to create a climate that facilitates harmonious development between all those involved.

SUMMARY

Encouraging good behaviour in children requires effort and planning. Adults must endeavour to create a climate and routine which is child-centred, stimulating and stable. If a room has plants and ornaments, for instance, there is little opportunity for children to move around freely. This can cause tension between the adult and child and, in turn, lead to conflict and upset.

As well as a suitable environment adults must have clear, simple rules. It is unfair for children to discover a rule only when they break it! Where a child has behaved inappropriately give immediate and clear feedback. Simply asking the child to 'be good' is not enough — what precisely do you mean by 'good'? The sanctions for inappropriate behaviour should reflect that behaviour and should follow it immediately. For instance, a three-year-old will not make the connection between her having hit a child at ten in the morning, and not receiving a sweet at four in the evening.

Some common problems with young children can be handled with careful thought and good communication between all those concerned with the child. Careful observation will allow the adult to judge what factors may be maintaining tearfulness at separation or causing the child to have a temper tantrum.

Aggression can take many forms — it may be the result of over-exuberance and a lack of awareness of strength or it may be a sign of a deeper problem of anger and conflict. Careful observation will give you a clue and you can act accordingly.

Quiet, withdrawn children need special attention — they need to be presented with opportunities to socialise and encouraged to explore and play with various materials. Some children are, by nature, loners. If a child is happy and thriving there is no need for concern.

Where children are considered 'bold' it is important to look closely at what behaviour is leading to this conclusion. Why are they behaving in this way? Perhaps they are angry, lonely, sad, frightened? Maybe adults are expecting too much of them, or too little? Perhaps there are difficulties at home? Perhaps there is a deeper, underlying problem that will need professional advice and support? Where a child is regarded as 'bold' adults need to take extra care in observing and looking beyond the behaviour in an effort to understand the message behind a child's actions.

EXERCISES

1. Visit a nursery or playgroup — your placement if appropriate — and ask about the policy for coping with unacceptable behaviour. Take time to observe: does the policy work? Would you change anything? If so, why?

2. List four simple rules you might have for a group of three to five-year-olds. How would you help them understand the rules? Be specific.

3. Select a partner and discuss why it is important to respond immediately to inappropriate behaviour rather than leave sanctions until later. Why is this less necessary with older children?

4. What are the settling procedures used in a nursery/playgroup that you visit? Do they differ with different age groups? Are parents free to visit as they wish? Are they free to stay with a child?

5. Why are temper tantrums common among two to four-year-olds? How are they best handled? How could you help a four-year-old cope with frustrations in a more appropriate way?

6. What are the possible explanations for aggressive behaviour? How might they affect the way you respond to different children?

7. Observe a group of children — note any inappropriate behaviours. Reading over your notes identify the factors that led to the behaviours; how was it maintained? Did anyone intervene? Was it necessary? What, if any, sanctions were used?

8. From your own experience with children discuss, with a partner, what situations are most likely to lead to unacceptable behaviour. Why? How might you alter the circumstances to help the child behave more appropriately?

9. Select a situation from above and carry out a role-play. Use different approaches to dealing with the difficult behaviour. Which works best? Which does not? Why?

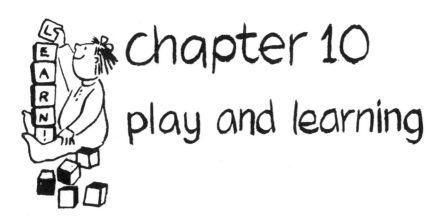

chapter 10
play and learning

One of the most common features of behaviour in childhood is play. We all have an understanding of what we mean by play and, particularly, what we mean when we talk of children playing. We all recognise to some degree that it is normal and healthy to play and the child who is not inclined to play may cause us concern. Despite the everyday nature of the concept of play we have a very poor understanding of the precise role of play in a child's life. We acknowledge that it occurs and that it must be important. But why is it important that children should be allowed the freedom to play? There have been a wide variety of theories proposed to explain the central nature of play in child development, ranging from the view that play was a way to work off surplus energy to the theory that it is through play that the child practises the skills necessary to become a successful adult. Consensus exists on the view that play is important but theories abound and controversy is plentiful.

Play is one of the essential experiences of childhood and the role of the adult in facilitating play, while at the same time allowing the child freedom to play, is a difficult one. Apart at all from the fun and enjoyment level, play is critical to a child's learning and style of future learning. Working with children gives us an opportunity to encourage and facilitate play so that it becomes, for the child, an enriching and educational experience. The chapter will describe and discuss the stages of play; the different types of play; some more recent theories of play; models of practice and how they view play and, finally, how best we can provide for play.

DEFINING PLAY

The word play has such a widespread use and meaning that there is some difficulty using it in the present context. How can I be sure that you, the reader, interpret play in the way I intend? The answer is that I cannot be sure. It is difficult for adults to understand what play means to the child. We have no means of remembering precisely what our own experience was, or what we gained from it. Many adults regard play as a pleasant means of passing the time and sometimes as a complete waste of time. Adults can trivialise play with expressions such as 'go out and play'; 'they are just playing'; 'you can play later, now it is time to work'. Others consider that any activity that a child does is play even where one might question how enjoyable the activity actually is for the child. How many of us recognise that play is a most essential factor in a child's development? Try and remember play: what were the characteristics that made it different from all other activities? It was fun, you were in charge, it was spontaneous and the rules seemed to evolve over time. It was harmonious and noisy, it was messy and tiring, it made you happy and you wanted more. This is how I remember play and yet when I look at practice in places focusing on play this is not always what I find. This is because the word play has broadened out to include 'fun' ways of learning, to include the more structured activities of form boards, jigsaws and educational games and to include those activities that the adult has planned for the children.

In early education play is seen as important. The development of the playgroup movement and the call for more early services for children reflects this recognition of the importance of early experiences and the role of play. There are differing views on the role that adults should play in this situation. Some argue that leaving children to their own devices and encouraging, but not interfering in play, is better than organising children's play and planning what they do during their time with the adult. A balanced, interactive method, with child-selected and adult-directed activities is best. One where, in the main, the child is in control of her own activity and learning. This does not mean that the adult sits and waits and only intervenes if there is an argument or a child is in danger. It means, rather, that the adult knows the children and their developmental levels. She knows what they can do, what they enjoy and she makes sure that the environment and materials meet their needs. She is present in an active way and can work with one child or a group as the need arises but not in a directive way. She is the architect of the opportunities for their experiences but she does not dictate those experiences.

The experiences of a young child in a playgroup or nursery should not mirror the experiences of the seven or eight-year-old in our primary school. The formal and directive methods used in classrooms is appropriate, in the main, with this older age group: it is quite inappropriate for the young child. The child is an active agent in her learning. The child under seven does not learn in the way older children and adults do. Rather she learns in a holistic and integrated way. By making a record player out of cardboard, paper and straws, the child is learning about shape, number, weight and balance. This learning is more valuable and more effective than if she was told that 'A straw won't balance there, it is too light — you would be better to use. . .'. The adults in her environment must facilitate this active involvement and be there to facilitate, encourage and support it but not to dictate the experience.

PLAY IS A PROCESS

The act of playing is often more important than the outcome. This separation of process (the doing) from the product (the outcome) can be difficult for adults. Why? As adults we tend to proceed through a process — A B C — towards a product. We read and study a book to acquire information that we will use to pass an examination, improve our practice, inform us of new matters or simply entertain us. We buy wool and a pattern to knit a jumper, wood and nails to make shelves. This order of plan/process/product is not at all typical of the way young children approach activities. For them the doing is more important than the arrival. Adults are often dismayed when children 'play about' with materials, waste them and make nothing of them. Adults measure achievement and success in terms of product, drawing a picture, building a house. In fact it appears that the process of play rather than the end product is more important to the child. The exploration, the observation, the experimentation — these all add to the learning. *To children the doing is the most crucial element in play.*

A young child starts to make a picture and gets carried away by the way the paint goes on to the paper and the table and the floor! Even where the product seems important the process still dominates. James was a three-year-old boy painting fish on to his picture. His fish were different colours. When they were painted he stood back thoughtfully and looked at his work. With a decisive movement he returned to the easel, took up a brush, dipped it in the pot of blue paint and covered his painting from top to bottom in blue paint. 'Look, look' he called 'fishes in the sea'. To the adult he had ruined his painting, it was just a mass of blue paint; to James, however, the process of painting took over from the act of representing and he was excited and satisfied by his 'doing'.

Too often adults can organise and plan activities that they feel children will enjoy and are surprised when this does not happen. In our effort to plan we may not allow the child to experience the essential process of the activity. In an effort to be efficient and effective we may end up taking away from children that very aspect of the activity that is critical — the experience of the process, the meeting with and overcoming of obstacles. Many art activities involve cutting and pasting. Certainly it is difficult for a four-year-old to cut out perfect circles but cutting is an important experience for children; it strengthens their fingers and assists the development of hand/eye co-ordination. Does it matter if the circles to be stuck on a card or a scene are irregular? In some cases it seems that it does because I have often seen adults cut the 'difficult' bits or provide circles already cut. In this instance all the child is doing is pasting someone else's circles, a less challenging activity than cutting and then pasting.

If we provide opportunities for children to create and we wish to display their work we must accept that children rarely represent things in the way adults do or might wish to. This is their right. If we try to hurry a child to production her learning will be shallow and this lack of depth takes from the value of the learning. Being forced to read too soon may yield a competent but reluctant reader. For the child who, through observing others read and through access to a variety of books and storytelling, comes to reading at her own pace, it is a treasure and a gift. An adult can put words on the ideas discovered by the child, but if she tries to tell a child what to think, the child will merely repeat what the adult says, with little interest or understanding.

STAGES OF PLAY

Stages of play have been studied from a social perspective; do children play differently with other children at different ages? It has also been studied in an effort to establish whether there are different types of play associated with different stages of thinking, that is cognitive development.

To take the subject of the social stages of play first. Any of you with the slightest experience of young children will acknowledge that young children are more likely to play on their own and older children enjoy playing in groups. Close observation will confirm this pattern.

Very young children are not at all social in their play, their play is *isolate/nonsocial play*. They interact alone with the objects and people in their environment but they do not play with anyone. Later this type of activity moves to *onlooker play* or *observer play*. Here the young child watches others at play and may, alone, imitate some of the behaviour observed. The child in the first year to eighteen months mainly plays at this *solitary* level.

As the child moves towards her second birthday she enjoys being in the company of other children. Hence the growth and popularity of mother and toddler groups. When observed it is clear that, although playing in the vicinity of other children, the young child at this stage still does not play with other children. Play at this stage has been called *parallel play*. This is a good label because you can observe children at, let us say, sand play. Two children appear to share the materials, that is one finishes with a spade and puts it down and the other child picks it up. They appear to be talking but close observation shows that each child is engaged in a monologue that does not necessarily include the other child.

This stage of play quickly moves on to what is called *social* or *co-operative play*. In many ways this is a misnomer because play at this stage of three to three-and-a-half can be anything but co-operative or social! Nonetheless it is true to say that the child is moving towards social play. Now she enjoys playing with others. Pretend and imaginative play often requires others. As the child gets older social play becomes more social as she is able to understand the needs of others as well as seeking to meet her own needs. Bruner and others have shown that children function at an intellectually higher level when in collaborative or co-operative situations than when playing alone. It has also been suggested that the quality of a child's play is enhanced by the presence, but not the interference, of a facilitating adult.

SOCIAL AND COGNITIVE STAGES OF PLAY

Age	Social	Cognitive
Birth–1 year	Isolate/nonsocial play	Early Practice play
1–2 years	Onlooker/observer play	Constructive/Mastery play
2–3 years	Parallel play	Early symbolic play
3–6 years	Social play	Symbolic play
6 years +		Games-with-rules

In looking at the different stages of play from the cognitive perspective we would expect to see differences across the ages that reflect the different reasoning abilities of children and this is indeed the case. The younger child's play is *functional/practice play*. That is, it involves pushing and pulling; putting in and taking out and lots of repetition. Children are practising their motor skills and gaining more control over them. Here too we see the enjoyment in games such as peek-a-boo. In such games children are laying down the foundation for turn-taking that is so important to many aspects of later behaviour, not least among them talking and listening. From this type of play they move on to *constructive/mastery play*. Here building and creating is important and reflects their growing ability in understanding cause and effect.

By the age of three, and often earlier, we see signs of the next identified stage of play, *symbolic* or *make-believe play*. This is the type of play we all recognise as play. Children taking on roles, pretending to be Daddy, the fireman, the nurse. It is also the stage where their art work and creative work in general begins to be more representational. That is, their trees look more like trees, although they may still be coloured in those magic variations that young children seem to enjoy. As the child's cognitive, reasoning skills move towards the more adult and abstract a further stage of play emerges. This stage is called *games-with-rules*. Children under the age of six begin to show an interest in games that have rules but are as yet unable to understand that rules are not flexible and that they exist for a reason. The ability to play co-operatively at games-with-rules reflects the child's ability to understand, to some degree, the reason for, and nature of rules and work within the boundary of rules. This stage is not reached until the age of six or seven and is not perfected until much later.

Recognising that there are different stages of social and cognitive play allows us to prepare the environment for children with this in mind by providing appropriate materials and opportunities. It means that our expectations are more realistic and that we can recognise a child whose play may not be emerging as one would expect and respond as we feel appropriate.

TYPES OF PLAY

Play takes diverse forms that change and become elaborated as the child matures. I find that in reading different authors you can find a wide variation in the types of play outlined.

Looking at the different types of play that children enjoy is valuable in that it can highlight what areas of development are being strengthened and, more importantly perhaps, what areas are being neglected. Changing forms of play may reflect newly-acquired abilities while the failure of play to evolve or become more complex may signal development problems. Children at play can enact and represent aspects of the world they may not be able to realise. By careful observation we can learn, for example, about children's concepts of social rules, understanding of the physical environment and their knowledge of language.

Physical play: As the name suggests this play involves the use of gross motor and fine motor skills. It is a form of play that is very common in young infants. They show vigorous physical activity when freed from the confines of cot, high chairs and buggies. When laid on the ground the baby will kick, roll, crawl and creep. Arms will wave and stretch and reach where there are stimulating objects to be touched. It is a type of play characterised by exploration, struggle, manipulation, adventure and practice. As children become mobile they practise walking, running, hopping and climbing. It is for this reason that large equipment and outdoor space is essential wherever children are cared for. Rough and tumble play where children play tag or chasing or 'fighting' is also a characteristic of physical play. The child loves to test out her skills and to overcome obstacles. She enjoys cycling and swinging and sliding and all those activities that help improve physical skills. You will recall that control over the physical self is a prerequisite to general self-control and self-confidence. As well as the gross motor skills this type of play also refers to those activities that challenge developments in the area of fine motor skills and hand/eye co-ordination such as threading beads, holding pencils and paint brushes, ball play, throwing and catching and so on.

Creative play: This type of play emerges early when the young child begins to play, or as we might say 'mess', with her food, play with sounds and also play with movements. The repetition of actions that we see here is rewarding for the child. As she gets older creative play, sometimes called messy play, moves on to include representational play such as drawing, painting, finger painting, pasting and collage. It also includes play with sand, water, clay, playdough and wood. This latter medium, wood, is rarely used in Ireland, perhaps because it is considered dangerous: I believe that with careful selection of material and with good supervision it is a very valuable play activity. Construction play with blocks, lego, meccano, boxes, crates and other waste material can also be an opportunity for creative play. Indeed the chance to create with large materials is something that should be encouraged as it requires physical development, co-operation and the use of imagination more so than some of the other activities outlined above.

Language play is also a characteristic of early creative play. Children play with words, create new ones, experiment with sound and make music, they indulge in long monologues and can find great 'jokes' in the sound of particular words.

Creative play also allows for the opportunity to 'play' with ideas and encourages the development of creative thinking. Creativity consists largely of re-arranging what we know in order to find out what we do not know and to think creatively we must be able to look afresh at what we usually take for granted. If not encouraged at an early age children will stop speculating and 'playing with ideas'.

Imaginative play: This is also a type of creative play but is considered separately because of its special importance in the lives of young children. Early attempts at imaginative play include making something — like a box — represent something else, such as a doll's cot. As the child reaches three it moves on to include role-taking. Here we catch a glimpse of the child's great skill in observation and imitation. By closely observing the child in the home corner or the Wendy House you may hear her speak like you or her mother and use expressions and gestures that she has seen others use. Through role play children often work out some understanding of the rules of their world and also practise some of the skills they are only beginning to acquire. The extension of this early role play is dressing up and presenting dramas and concerts. This type of play also matures to include private fantasy games, often with specific rules, between children that can last for days on end. This is more typical of the older child.

Structured play: Here we are referring to play that is governed by the material used rather than by the child herself. Building blocks that have outlined windows, doors and arches, for instance, are more appropriately placed in this category of play than under the constructive creative play outlined above. Here also we include jigsaws, puzzles, matching games and a wide range of what are called educational toys. Certain art activities fit in under this category rather than under creative play and these include such things as insets, stencils and outlines. Games with rules such as ludo, lotto, and later draughts and chess, can also be included in this category.

Free play: This is perhaps the most difficult type of play to describe and yet it has been considered to be the most important in young children's development. It is really that type of play where children have freedom, choice and control. It can include creative and imaginative play, aspects of physical play and games-with-rules: the rules, however, are negotiated by the children playing. It is free of adult guidance, direction and constraint although the adult should be vigilant and may, at times and only on request, become involved. It is not a chaotic, anarchic type of play, it has its boundaries but it is truly child-led, spontaneous and free.

PLAY AT DIFFERENT AGES

Children show signs of playfulness in their behaviour from a very early age. Young infants will imitate simple actions and by the second half of their first year will playfully imitate sounds they hear. Below is a rough guide to the types of play that may be observed in children at different ages. Naturally there is flexibility in this list. Older children often enjoy the opportunity to play with bricks and water activities more associated with a younger age group. This can happen when they are tired or if they have a particular plan; they should not be stopped simply because an adult thinks it is 'babyish'.

0–1-year-olds: Infants play by looking and listening. They kick, rattle and grasp at objects and later they bite at them and drop them. Indeed this is often turned into a game if someone picks the object up, as down it goes again! Children also play with texture and they like to cuddle and be cuddled.

1–2-year olds: Now the child is becoming mobile and enjoys pushing and pulling, scribbling and crayoning (with large, easy-flow crayons). They like to build, to put things in and take them out. They enjoy being in the company of others and looking at bright picture books.

2–3-year-olds: At this stage children enjoy sorting, stacking, threading, hammering, drawing, dressing-up, simple jigsaws, sand, water, playdough, building play, paint, playing in the presence of other children, listening to stories and looking at pictures.

3–5-year-olds: By the age of three children enjoy all the above, plus playing with others; make-believe and pretend play, music-making, dancing, cutting-out, modelling, stories (to hear and to read), painting, baking, construction toys, balls, rackets, miniature toys.

5–8-year-olds: Now children enjoy all the above and social play with playlets and concerts that they devise. They like reading, finding out, doing new things, challenges.

The above is a guide to the activities that children enjoy at different ages. At two a child who won't put the pegs in their proper holes or who throws the puzzle about or fiddles with the cards is not bold or bored but is saying 'I am not interested in playing with these toys *yet*, there are other things I want to do first'. A knowledge of the approximate ages at which to expect different types of play and an understanding of the children with whom you work will allow you to make the most likely interpretation and act accordingly.

WHY DO CHILDREN PLAY?

In the last century Herbert Spencer proposed that children play to work off surplus energy: adults, he believed, used up their energy in their work. Groos, at the turn of the century, proposed that it was through play that children practise the skills they will need later on in life. Indeed the pretend play of children does help them learn new skills. Anna Freud, drawing from the psychodynamic theory of her father, saw a therapeutic value in play. Where children were faced with fears or conflicts they would, she believed, work them out through play. There is something to be said for each of the above explanations and the many others that have been put forward. The subject is well treated by Tina Bruce in her book *Time to Play in Early Childhood Education*. Bruce believes that play has an integrating function — that is, through play children find out new information, re-arrange old knowledge, integrate and practise in play and through this process they learn more about their world.

Play, it could be said, is the way children come to understand their world and their position in it. Child's play is of value to the child in the here and now, it is fun and useful for its own sake. It does, however, also have a value for the child in the longer term. For example it helps the development of vocabulary and conversational skills and of social skills such as waiting, sharing and turn-taking. Through play children can improve their powers of observation, concentration and explanation. Play helps children discover different methods of finding out and problem-solving. It is through their play that children begin to understand the fact that different people might feel different emotions, have a different view of the world; children develop a sense of empathy, they begin to develop a more complete view of their world as their horizons widen and their experiences deepen. Play also facilitates the development of skills such as hand control, body control and hand/eye co-ordination. Through play children also pick up, informally, knowledge about colours, numbers, letters, symbols and signs.

IS ALL PLAY VALUABLE?

Play can be rich, exciting, motivating and exhausting or it can be boring and tedious. Parry and Archer studied play and identified two levels. Of these two

179

levels they wrote: 'One merely keeps children occupied; the other contributes to their educational development. The difference between the two levels of play is not easy to detect. Play can sometimes look good with children actively involved, and yet lack the elements which contribute towards educational growth'. There is an assumption in early education that the full development of the child depends only on her opportunity to play. This is an unrealistic view of the role of play. It is undoubtedly a central activity for the young child but it must be of high quality and wide variety in order to meet its potential in the development of the child.

Play has fallen into disrepute by appearing to be all things to all children, by being regarded as either a child's work or something to do after the important things in life have been done. With no rigorous theoretical underpinning this allows other educators to question the value of play and to fuel the move towards the more traditional adult-led education of bygone days. Play is important but it may not be all that is important. One of the authors who has been critical of the simple acceptance that all play is good for children is Corinne Hutt. In her book, *A Natural History of the Preschool: Exploration, Play and Learning*, she looks in detail at the claims made for play and argues that there is more than play in children's lives. For example she separates out *exploring* from *play*. She argues that exploring is asking the question 'what does this do?' while play is asking a different question 'what can I do with this?' Both are important. Extending this argument Hutt goes on to say that while play is an important element in learning it is not the only way a child learns and in the early years learning is a close combination of exploration and play.

Others, following on from Groos, have argued that play is the principal means of learning during the early years; it helps the development of abilities necessary for future success; it is pleasurable; it fosters personal and social development; it acts as a medium for the transmission of cultural beliefs and it develops the ability to think and to use information and knowledge. Whichever view you hold in relation to the relative importance of play to learning in the early years it is clear that play has an important role and the opportunity to play must be made available to all our children.

PROVIDING FOR PLAY

Studies by Sylva and her colleagues suggest that, while some adults agree with the importance of play in early years, at the same time they provide a service that is directive and adult-led rather than child-centred. There are many possible explanations for the discrepancy between expressed opinion and practice and one that I believe is particularly important, and difficult to overcome, is that the experiences we adults have had as young children direct our behaviour with children more than we expect.

Appropriate experiences: Our increased understanding of child development allows us recognise that children learn best, and gain more valuable knowledge and information, through having active encounters with the world. They process this information in a meaningful way and come to understand the world more thoroughly. When planning for children we must take account of their development level and provide more *developmentally appropriate* activities and materials. The pre-reading and pre-writing exercises used in primary schools are not developmentally appropriate to young children. Because children want, in the main, to please adults they will match pictures to pictures and colour in the various outlines but may learn very little from the experience. They will learn more about reading and writing by using, and seeing used, reading and writing materials. We all learn better when we understand the meaning of what we are learning and recognise the context.

Adequate space: We must also ensure that we provide adequate space, both indoors and outdoors so that children are free to move. There are services in Dublin where the space has been so confined that babies have to spend their days in buggies or high chairs. This is very unsatisfactory and does not allow for the normal development of physical skills. It also compromises the type of social and interactive contact the babies can have with other children and adults.

Sufficient time: As well as space we must also consider the provision of time. It is of little value to allow children plan an activity and set about it only to be told that it is now 'tidy-up time'. Children have only a vague awareness of time and they cannot grasp the idea of, say, five minutes. We must help children develop a sense of time by being concrete in the way we talk of the passage of time. There must be some order on the day but flexibility to allow children the time to complete an activity is also important.

Young children are ready and anxious to please and learn certain things through imitation. It is possible, through regular practice and repetition, for four-year-olds to recite tables and letters. This performance may be gratifying to adults but it cannot be considered as learning — we know that children at this age are not capable of making sense of these abstract symbols and the concepts underlying them. Why do we lay such great store on telling? Take this book, for instance. In writing it I have brought together a range of facts and information for the reader to study and assimilate. It will only become meaningful when the reader has practice upon which to base the information. One can write about competent infants, volatile two-year-olds, questioning three-year-olds in volumes but it means little except, perhaps, passing an examination, until you own the *knowledge* through your experiences and the guidance of this and other books. Knowing grows from within, from internalised experience. So it is with your learning: it is even more so with the young child.

What we attempt to 'teach' children may not be what they learn. Because they enjoy pleasing adults they will try, they will perform but they are developmentally unable to learn symbolically at this early stage. Received learning through symbolic and verbally presented concepts will only come at a later stage of cognitive development. With so many things to be learned how can we believe that the adult can make the selection of facts a child must know? In the end it is the child who will have to work out her own future.

Allowing the child the freedom to learn through her own activity does not mean leaving a child rudderless in an environment full of things to do. There must be a plan, a structure, but this should be within the mind of the adult rather than visible in a static, predictable routine. Material must be well-organised and understanding the child's general development on all fronts, not just cognitive, is essential. To avoid children's play becoming low level and desultory the adult has to become a part of the system. Bruner found that when there was a facilitating adult in the area where children were playing, their play was of a higher level of complexity than when children were 'working' with adults or playing where there was no adult nearby.

Through dialogue between children and adults, the learning which has occurred during the exploratory phase becomes the focus of conversation and the adult can provide whatever the children need to take their learning further, whether this be providing new or different equipment, asking questions and giving ideas or help with planning and investigation. This does not mean strict adult direction and adult planning in what the child will, for instance, learn from water play next Tuesday. Rather we are talking about a sensitive adult, confident in her knowledge of child development, confident in her knowledge of the children in her care, being observant and child-led in how she responds to a particular situation; an adult who avoids what Parry and Archer have identified as the level of play which just keeps children occupied, by providing challenging experiences and encouraging play that contributes to their development. This idea of the adult as facilitator to the child is not new and earlier this century, L. Vygotsky, a psychologist with particular interest in child development, wrote that 'what the child can do today in co-operation, tomorrow he will be able to do alone'.

DIFFERENT MODELS OF EARLY EDUCATION

Despite consensus on the importance of the early years and the role of play in learning there is active debate about how best to foster learning, e.g. what method or approach is best for children. Is one method the best? How should the environment be structured? How much should adults intervene? How much activity should be child-led? How should these early experiences reflect the needs of formal education? Below are described some of the principles underlying different practice.

The major models of early education that exist can be classified as:

The social/traditional model: This owes a great deal to the pioneering work of Froebel and the legacy of the McMillan sisters and Susan Isaacs who worked in England during the early part of this century. This model stresses the notion of child-centred education in a nurturing environment. The emphasis in programmes such as this is on social development and maturation. The environment is planned to help children learn through playful experiences. Many of our preschools and playgroups reflect this philosophy in their practice.

The academic model: Here the emphasis is on formal structured provision with the aim of developing the skills necessary for school success. Such programmes are not typical in Ireland but do exist in the US and often emphasise the development of language. This reflects the belief that children who fail at school do so because they have a poorer facility with language and literacy than their more successful peers. This model of provision is often aimed at improving the skills of the 'disadvantaged' child so that they might succeed in their formal education and centres on the belief that 'some things must be learned'. It is very structured and the adults often use a specific textbook.

The sensori/cognitive model: The most well-known model in this group is the Montessori method, discussed earlier. This method emphasises the importance of sensory stimulation in the early years of learning. The child works in a planned environment at her own pace. Material is carefully designed to meet the different needs of children at different stages and the child's progress through the programme is 'object directed' rather than adult directed. The adult is seen as a resource and her title, directress, reflects the role to be taken.

The constructivist model: This model of provision takes the development of thinking and the problem solving skills of the child as its focus. It follows the Piagetian view of development and highlights the child's need to be an active agent in her learning and to construct her own reality through active engagement with materials and play opportunities. The most widely known example is the High/Scope method which encourages children to plan their activities, carry them out and review them. In this way children become more aware of their thinking and, it is believed, will develop more efficient and effective thinking skills.

DOES THE TYPE OF MODEL MATTER?

Research carried out in the US by the High/Scope Educational Foundation suggests that, in the short to medium term, *any* good quality programme, run by well qualified and supported staff, will yield positive results for the children attending. There appears to be no difference of effect between the approaches. More recent results of longitudinal study into the Perry Preschool Project (a High/Scope programme) indicate that, by nineteen years of age, more children who followed this programme finished school, less required special or remedial education during their schooling, less got into trouble with the law and there were fewer teenage pregnancies outside of stable relationships when compared to those who followed other programmes or attended no early educational service.

The primary difference between the Perry Preschool Project and other models of provision is that it encourages the child to take control of her thinking and gives the child more opportunity to explore and learn from self-initiated experiences. However, the sample in the High/Scope study was very small and it is difficult to generalise results from a small sample. An evaluation of children attending High/Scope nurseries found them to be more independent learners, to spend less time in aimless wandering and to be less disruptive than similar children in more traditional nurseries. It is worth pointing out, however, that a great deal can occur while a child is aimlessly wandering and 'wasting' time. It is important not to expect too much in the line of activity from children and not to measure success too firmly in relation to school or academic success. If we do this we may take away the essential ingredients of childhood.

Other studies from Britain have found that aspects of provision such as room organisation, availability of resources and a high degree of good quality interaction between children and adults also contribute to good quality programmes as measured by the behaviour of children. Children from such programmes were better able to cope in primary school, were more independent, showed greater complexity of play, had longer concentration spans and better use of the teacher as a resource than children from preschools constrained by limited space, time and opportunity to play and learn.There has been little published research on this subject in Ireland but at the time of writing there is an evaluation of a High/Scope programme being carried out at a Dublin daycare centre and the results should be published by the mid 1990s.

Despite the apparently positive results of the High/Scope study, it is difficult to come down categorically in favour of any one particular method over another. As there are so many variables involved, it is complex to unravel all the interacting links. Osborn and Milbank, in their comprehensive review of early educational services in Britain, found that, undoubtedly, preschool experience is beneficial to young children. It is possible to say that if we want our young children to grow up able to adapt to change, make decisions, communicate clearly and effectively and contribute to society we must ensure that our practice is enabling and developmentally appropriate. That it encourages and challenges the child to explore, create, discover, problem-solve and communicate. To do this adults must plan and structure the environment for children. Structure does not mean a tightly-run routine; it means, rather, an invisible, cohesive structure where there is room for routine, pacing, individualisation and integration.

Working with young children we must always be open to reviewing practice and old familiar habits. While acknowledging the necessity for some order and routine — and indeed what value is it to the child in the long run not to introduce some routine — it is also important to understand the child's perspective. Because we are adults and recognise the value of routine, focusing on an alternative may be difficult. Let us look at the child. Her day is a flowing from one experience to another — she does not timetable the day. She gets absorbed in one activity and does not want to stop. Yet how often do we interrupt to say 'it's time to . . .' and then regret the lack of interest, lack of enthusiasm or poor concentration we find for the new or next activity? How often have you found yourself saying — 'I should have let them at it'? Does it really matter that you get to read the story you had planned before lunch? Surely another opportunity will arise.

If child-centred education means anything, it stands for a way of life for the child which will enable her to develop fully as the person she is. Play is a process that allows the child to explore novelty, practise skills and integrate new information. It is the process through which she comes to understand the world and her place in it. It is the process which allows her to take control of herself and her life. As adults we have an important role in stimulating and facilitating play. The importance of personal relationships cannot be over-emphasised. All the people a child meets are in some way responsible for shaping her development and the people she comes to love and admire influence her most of all. What she becomes as a person is, in large part, a result of what she learns. She and others are interactive in this learning. We must not abuse our powerful role by deciding what it is children must do and rendering play no more than a meaningless title put on activities owned, not by the child, but by the adult. True play belongs to the child.

SUMMARY

Play is a central characteristic of early childhood behaviour. It is the process through which young children come to understand their world and their position in it.

Play follows a developmental path and there are clearly distinguishable stages of play. These stages can be considered in terms of: *Social characteristics* where the child moves from isolated play through to social play and, *Cognitive characteristics* where play develops from simple practice play, through symbolic play to games-with-rules.

There are many theories about why children play. They range from the very early view that play works off excess energy to the more recent theories that see play as a way of practising skills and dealing with fears. No one theory satisfactorily explains the reasons for play.

When providing for play adults must consider:

• the developmental appropriateness of materials and activities

• the degree to which children have control over their play

• the time and space allowed to children for their play.

In working with young children one is providing an early years curriculum, a series of experiences and activities, based, in general, on the belief that children learn best through play. The different models of early education outlined in this chapter are informed by different views of how children play and learn. Understanding these different perspectives can assist you in evaluating your own practice and in assessing your aims for young children and their development.

EXERCISES

1. List the social stages of play. Compare these stages with the cognitive stages of play.

2. Describe the difference between the play of a two-year-old and a three-year-old.

3. Write a short essay in which you define play and present a brief review of some of the more common theories of play.

4. What are the main types of play? Visit a nursery or playgroup. Are opportunities for each type of play available? Are they available at all times? If not — how could such provision be made?

5. List the four models of early education outlined in this chapter — select two and discuss them in more detail with a partner.

6. (a) Plan a play opportunity that is developmentally appropriate for a group of normal three to five-year-olds.

    (b) Take the above activity and modify it so that it is developmentally appropriate for a group of three to five-year-olds with speech delay.

7. Write an essay starting: 'Children play because ...'

chapter 11
applying developmental knowledge

When we talk about early childhood and the theory that influences our practice we must include in the discussion the issue of education. Indeed throughout the text I have made reference to early education in the context of working with young children. The experiences of early childhood, whether gained solely in the home or from a variety of settings, serve as an important educational experience for children.

To observe early child development is to observe a series of triumphs for informal education, but education nonetheless; the repetition to achieve an end, the original and creative errors of language as the child explores it and attempts to find the rules. Children show curiosity and commitment in their early learning. The foundations for future education are laid down in the open, curious, exploring and social play of young children. The challenge for those of us working in early childhood education is, as Margaret Donaldson pointed out in her excellent book *Children's Minds*, 'to understand how something that began so well can often end so badly' for so many children.

The Green Paper on Education, *Education for a Changing World*, presents twelve educational aims. The first nine of them will strike a chord with anyone working with young children and confirm for them the critical importance of their job. The aims are introduced and identified as follows:

'In a relatively homogeneous society such as Ireland's, a reasonable consensus might be anticipated on the broad educational aims. . . . The following summary of aims are proposed as the basis for such consensus:

- Fostering an understanding and critical appreciation of the values — moral, spiritual, social and cultural — of the home and society generally.

- Promoting self-esteem and self-worth, combined with a respect for the rights and beliefs of others.

- Fostering intellectual development and the attainment of one's full educational potential.

- Developing a spirit of inquiry and the capacity for the critical and constructive analysis of issues.

- Developing expressive and creative abilities to the individual child's full capacity.

- Providing students with the necessary skills to equip them for work and to enable them to function effectively in society.

- Creating tolerant, caring and politically aware members of society.

- Fostering a spirit of self-reliance, of innovation and of enterprise.

- Creating an environment that is conducive to and supportive of emotional and physical well-being.

- Achieving standards of educational performance comparable to the highest internationally.

- Ensuring that people are appropriately educated and trained to support the country's economic development.

- Ensuring that Ireland's young people acquire a keen awareness of their national and European heritage and identity.

There can be little argument that good quality early services for children would also aim to achieve the above.

PLANNING FOR WORKING WITH YOUNG CHILDREN

What is your aim in working with young children? How can you achieve this aim for children as individuals and in the context of the group?

Goals: Selecting activities and drafting routine is basic to planning for children, even where your responsibility is only to a small number of children or to very young children. This needs careful thought and planning. Activities must be both interesting and appropriate to the abilities of the children and their developmental stages. Planning will require careful observation. In your planning you must consider who you are planning for, what you are planning for and how you will achieve your aims. Goals set must be realistic and specific, not vague ideas about what children need. Plans will not be successful if they are over-ambitious or if they are unplanned and too simple. Where plans do not go smoothly the failures must be discussed. Persevere, share ideas and continue to plan and evaluate your practice. This is more valuable to children and more stimulating for the adults and in all provides for a much better quality of service. Your efforts to select goals should not lead to an overly adult-led, adult-dominated service.

It is generally agreed that early services must meet the needs of young children and that this must be done in collaboration with all those concerned with the particular child. What are the needs of children in the early years? A useful guide to the basic needs of children has been outlined by Mia Kellmer Pringle in her book *The Needs of Children*. Basic needs for all children include the following:

- The need for *basic physical care,* such as the need for protection, food, rest, hygiene and shelter.

- The need for *affection*, including physical contact with holding, kissing, admiration, tenderness, approval, patience, making allowances and general concern and understanding.

- The need for *security*, manifest by continuity of care, stability in family structure and daily care, a predictable environment with consistent patterns of routine and simple rules consistently applied.

- The need for *stimulation of potential*, by praise, attention, and encouragement of exploration and curiosity. Also important here is one's responsiveness to questions and the guiding of skills development, through providing opportunity for play and education.

- The need for *guidance and control*, where the child is helped acquire appropriate social behaviours. This involves management and discipline, taking account of the child's level of understanding. This requires patience and respect for the child on the part of the adult.

- The need for *responsibility*, in line with the developmental ability of the child. To begin with one should give responsibility in small areas such as self-care, tidying up playthings or clothes and later in allowing the child be responsible for certain decisions which help him or her learn from mistakes as well as successes.

- The need for *independence*, a need which begins to manifest itself as early as the first year. Independence with protection and not overprotection is important. Overprotection is as bad as giving too much responsibility too soon; both put pressure on a child and can lead to difficulties.

Most people planning services for the young child do so in the context of these needs. The nature of the service provided can have a profound impact on the development of the child's self-image, self-esteem and self-concept. Children acquire different ways of thinking about themselves and the type of service provided can affect this by either encouraging a mastery orientation in the child or a learned helplessness. The former is to be recommended.

INVOLVING PARENTS

The focus of your planning is the child and the quality of the service to the child. In this context the fact that you are sharing the care of children with their parents must be taken into account. Why involve parents? Parents have rights and these rights should include a clear understanding of what is happening to their children when in the care of others. It is important to recognise the fact that parental involvement should be included in the planning, and that account of to what level this can be achieved, will vary from circumstance to circumstance.

Children accomplish a great deal of their learning informally. They learn from the people they meet, the things they see and hear, the experiences they have and the impact of their parents and homes. If we are to maximise children's learning we must respect the contribution parents make to the process. Even where we are providing early services for children and families in need or at risk we must not assume that we are compensating for ineffective parenting and are in a better position than parents. We are in a different position to parents but we must recognise that under certain circumstances we could all be poor or ineffective parents. Most parents are trying to do the best for their children. Many parents are anxious to know how their children are progressing and welcome the opportunity to discuss how they might help this process. But they may need the opportunity for this type of interaction to be made available to them in an explicit way. Parents may not know how to go about discussing their children's progress and may say nothing rather than appear to be checking up on staff. They may feel that it is not their business to ask what happens during the day or to comment on their child's behaviour. Parents may also feel that, as trained personnel, staff know much more than parents. This perception needs to be overcome. Trained staff have much information to share with parents but also have a lot to learn from parents. The process should be one of partnership between all those caring for the the child's best benefit.

Many parents may not be fully aware of the rapidity and variety of their children's learning. They can see the rapidity of their growth and measure it in terms of the need for new shoes or clothes but not so with development in other areas. Few parents realise that young children, for instance, think differently. They may recognise that their three-year-old has a will of her own but may not realise that what she will be as a mature person will, to some degree, be affected by the way adults handle and respond to her behaviour at this early age.

LISTENING TO PARENTS

Parents can provide valuable information and insight into individual children themselves and staff should be willing to listen and respond to this. By encouraging openness with parents you also support the opportunity for parents to come together and learn from one another. Time spent with parents is a good investment; all we do with children outside the home must dovetail with what she brings with her from home and what she will continue to learn from home. The importance of parental involvement is recognised by those who provide more formal education. The recent evolution of the National Parents Council and the development of the Home/School Liaison Programme is evidence of this recognition. In the recent Green Paper, *Education for a Changing World*, we find the following relevant quotes:

'Since parents are the primary educators of their children, their representatives have a critical role to play in the management of schools and in supporting the education of their children in school.'

Of more immediate relevance, perhaps, to those of us concerned with the development of early childhood services is the statement found on page 135 of the Green Paper that:

'Experience of the Home/School Liaison Programme has confirmed the importance of achieving the involvement of parents with the school at as early a stage as possible in the child's development. It is proposed, therefore, to extend the development of preschool programmes as part of the Home/School Liaison Programme for disadvantaged areas. . . .'

Parental involvement can occur at different levels depending on the service provided. The evolution of the preschool playgroup movement occurred as a direct commitment to the involvement of parents in providing early experiences for their children. In these services parents are actively involved in planning, fundraising and providing the service to their children. Where you are caring for the children of working parents it is not always possible to include the parents in the everyday running of the service but every effort must be made to keep them well informed. Parents should feel free to come into your house or nursery, they should have access to the play and sleep areas used by the children and be free to comment on any aspect of the care given. By keeping a brief record on each child each day to give to the parents they can be made feel a part of the system and not excluded. This is particularly useful with the very young child as it allows parents the opportunity to note the daily pattern of their child's behaviour. Parents can be asked to assist in different ways. For example they can be asked to help out at parties and outings, to provide junk material, to fundraise or to become active in the management of the service. The onus is on the providers of the service to make parents feel welcome, to keep them informed and to encourage their participation in this aspect of the care of their child.

THEORY INTO PRACTICE

This book has presented an introduction to aspects of child development and early education that should allow a deeper understanding of the child. Its value will be in how this information translates into practice. While providing materials and situations appropriate to the needs and interests of children is important to their development, it is by no means all that is needed. What children do with the materials in the situations provided is also important. Researchers and observers of early childhood provision have frequently criticised practice as being developmentally inappropriate, see, particularly, Tricia David's *Under Five — Under-Educated?*

There is a tendency to expect too much of young children in terms of our ambitions of what they should be able to do and how they should be able to behave. But at the same time we may expect too little — 'I'll pour the juice as you might spill it'. There is little research on practice available from Ireland, but from the little there is, we do not seem to be any different to our European and American neighbours in this regard. There is a need on the part of early educators, even those, perhaps especially those, working with the very young, to be systematic in their planning of the environment so that the child's experiences are worthwhile rather than simply occupying. You will recall that Parry and Archer suggested that play can be at two levels — simply occupying or developmentally challenging. As practitioners it is important to plan for our work with young children in such a way that allows the child to experience a challenging environment while at the same time ensuring that the climate is supportive and not too demanding.

There is some danger in talking about planning. It suggests aims, objectives, goals, structures and so on. In the wrong or inexperienced hands this could lead to an overly adult-directed, product-oriented provision. We have already discussed the fact that process is often much more important, and valuable, to the young child than the end product. We need to trust that children will learn if they are allowed to explore, question and plan in their own play. This is not to advocate a child-dominated situation where the adult is no more than an observer. Not at all. It is to emphasise the fact that the role of the adult is one of facilitating children in their play so that they can have a good deal of control over the experience, so that they can actively explore, play and learn and so that it is they that own the learning and not the adult. Where the adult is in control of the learning the child will perform but it is difficult to assume that she will learn.

We must recognise in ourselves the tendency to want visible outcome from an activity, order and concentration during an activity and we must ask ourselves why? While seeking the reassuring results which adult-led art activities, stencil and inset work, work books and work cards can bring, many everyday opportunities presented by the environment or the individual child to learn the same things — in a more meaningful context — get pushed aside. While what is learned may be sound enough what could have been learned may never be known. There are certain dangers in formulating aims and objectives for our practice. The perceived emphasis on the social and emotional aspects of development has been seen as a weakness of preschool provision as it is considered to ignore the cognitive aspect of development. This is to ignore the whole inter-relationship between aspects of development particularly the cognitive aspects of emotional/social development.

Audrey Curtis, in her book *A Curriculum for the Preschool Child*, has identified seven broad areas of skills and competencies that should be fostered in young children and which should inform the planning and development of any early years curriculum. The approach of the adult should be to develop the curiosity of the child and encourage her to become motivated from within. This can be done through the provision of appropriate materials, well laid-out space and sufficient opportunity and time to play.

You will notice how closely the points outlined below reflect a number of the points raised by the Green Paper on Education. Our practice should foster:

- The development of self-awareness.

- The development of social skills — affiliation skills, co-operation, resolution of conflict, kindness and caring.

- The development of cultural awareness skills.

- The development of communication skills — through language, music, movement and art.

- The development of motor and perceptual skills.

- The development of analytical and problem-solving skills.

- The development of aesthetic/creative awareness — art, music, literature.

Particularly in early years provision the decisions about what to make available in a programme should be made with reference to the child — emphasising the process and the meaningfulness of what we are trying to present. Children can learn about numbers when that learning is grounded in the concrete reality of objects. The young child learns more by doing than by being told, but this doing needs to be within a meaningful context. 'Context-bound' learning starts the child on the developmentally appropriate path towards the 'context-free', or abstract, disembedded, thought of the adult. It is the context that brings the child and content (knowledge) together. The skills, knowledge, concepts and attitudes to be acquired are part of the activities provided by the adult. If we start from a disembedded perspective — dealing, say, with the numerical symbol of four (4), the young child may learn about four, but will lack the active experience of four she would gain by counting out the number of children in a group and then getting the correct number of cups for snack-time. We cannot *teach* concepts of numbers to young children. These come by reason of the children's growth and concrete experiences of the world and we cannot hasten this coming.

CHOOSING FOR CHILDREN

An author who believes that while, on the one hand we may be providing inappropriate experiences for children, on the other hand we are not challenging them enough is Tricia David, mentioned above. She believes that, while we might wish to extend their development we may in fact be inhibiting this development. She points out that children need to learn in a cross-curricular fashion, that is they can learn about the number four through their painting, a story, preparation for snack-time, a look at nature and so on. There are opportunities at all times and adults must be alert to these and use them. She also stresses the fact that children need to form links between the facts they discover. This is true of adults also. You will find that learning theory is much easier when you have some practical experience to back it up. Children also need to have their learning reinforced through exposure to a wide variety of experiences. David writes:

'Where children are offered activities which foster exploration and first-hand experience through play, and opportunity to reflect on those experiences — with other children and adults — they will be gaining a firm foundation for their future education.'

Adults should know *why* a certain activity is provided and *how* it might benefit a particular child. This is where observation, understanding of child development and your knowledge of the individual child come together. Sensitivity to a child's needs and interests can inform the provision of appropriate opportunities. We must move away from the idea that a child must first learn what we have to teach her and then she will be able to do things for herself and change this to allow the child do it for herself and then expand what she has experienced in dialogue with her.

IMPROVING PRACTICE AND MEETING DIFFERENT DEVELOPMENTAL NEEDS

We communicate through gesture, movement, spoken and written word. Symbols are an important element in communication. Throughout the early years — as language both spoken and written begins to emerge as the predominant form of communication — other non-verbal forms of communication are still used and of critical importance. These non-verbal skills include gesture, movement, mime, body language. Our world is full of symbols and the opportunity to experience these and draw on the experiences is important for children.

Literacy: From early on symbols play an important role. At a very early age children show signs of recognising letters and signs. At almost three my daughter shouted 'Look, me, me' as we passed a bus. I thought she had seen her reflection in the window as we passed the bus but when it happened again I realised that she was referring to an advertisement on the side of the bus for a breakfast cereal that had the letter K prominently in its name. My daughter's name is Katie and even at this early age she was showing an emerging literate ability. She identified the letter K as herself. By four and five children are familiar with a wide variety of symbols that represent objects and information. These include visual symbols such as road signs, diagrams, advertisements, maps, numbers, pictures, letters and also auditory symbols such as buzzers, whistles, bells. There is a difference between recognising symbols and understanding them, and how we come to handle symbols follows a developmental path. In the beginning children perceive differences (discriminate) and similarities and tend to classify at a simple level, grouping like symbols and objects together. Higher level classification and seriation skills emerge as the child becomes older. Initially children tend to put letters and numbers together but by four they can clearly distinguish between letters and numbers. You can teach a three-year-old to repeat C-A-T spells CAT, but they don't understand it and may say, if shown the word CAT — 'oh yes, a pussy!'

Mathematics: Mathematics is also a form of communication and includes aspects of measurement, shape and number. The understanding of mathematical concepts is tied into development. The following examples of mathematical thinking in a four-year-old and a child of almost seven illustrate the point:

- Katie, on her fourth birthday, said: 'I'm four today — I'm nearly five'.

- Clare, at six years and nine months made the following observation: 'Ali is three today, so this is her fourth birthday — you know, when you count her actual birth day.'

You will recall that it is not until well into the pre-operational period that children grasp the concept of conservation of volume, and the concept of time is not well developed until the child reaches seven or eight. It is an abstract notion and very difficult for children to grasp. 'At night', 'now', 'tomorrow' can have many different meanings and 'yesterday' can mean any time in the past. Rhymes and repetitious stories are important to help the child develop the sense of time. The younger child enjoys picture books that show the passage of time such as the sequences outlined in 'My Day' and later the story 'What time is it, Mr Wolf?'

A sense of time: To help the development of an awareness of duration, visible assistance like an egg timer, alarm clock, cooker buzzer with the explicit statement — 'it takes four minutes from boiling for a soft-boiled egg' is helpful. A sound notion of duration takes a long time to develop. Clock faces are not very valuable unless real and linked to concrete events. Days of the week, weather charts, chore schedules help to establish time-related ideas but a child of five will still have difficulties, developmentally, in understanding the invariant and temporal nature of the days of the week, despite the fact that she might rhyme them off.

Social skills: Children learn to co-operate with one another by working co-operatively together (a situation which may require adult guidance) and not by being taught 'good manners' and 'obedience'. When context is clear children are more likely to understand what the rules are and why they exist. Dramatic or pretend play affords excellent opportunities for the creation of a good social atmosphere. During their early years children are not well equipped with social skills. They are still learning and one of the roles of the adults in their lives is to assist the emergence of prosocial skills. Persuading, forcing and even expecting a child to be helpful may be unrealistic. The child must experience respect and helpfulness, if she is to become helpful. Guiding children in being helpful can encourage children, e.g. 'Mary is having difficulty tidying all those toys away — can you help her, Sonia?' or 'Oh! I left my book on the shelf — can you get it for me John?' Merely bringing children together will not help them socialise. Planned assistance and good modelling are essential.

Self-control: Emotions have a powerful influence on behaviour. Emotional maturity is something towards which we all strive but it is important not to expect it too soon. Children depend on adults to provide a stable environment in which feelings can mature. Asking a child to behave 'like a four-year-old', when she's only just reached four is overly ambitious! Saying things like 'well you must stop crying, you're a big girl now, you're four' gives little guidance to the child on how to manage the feelings that are causing the tears and may just confirm for the child her inadequacy. The emotional experience of the moment is the one that counts most, so telling a crying child that her mother will be back after snack-time doesn't take away the feeling of desertion. As a culture we tend to rush children towards maturity, proudly expressing a child's being 'advanced for her age'. We must let a child be her age — not an easy task. When we have put a lot of effort into preparing a story and find that our group are fidgeting and squirming we may feel resentful that the children are not appreciative of our efforts — but children don't know that we may expect them to appreciate our efforts!

Encouraging creativity: Most adults working with young children foster their creative inclinations. There are many adults, however, who decide for the child what it is she will make or create. The results are put on show and anything else may be considered waste. Children will not always put creative materials to 'good' use. You may know that there is only a little gold paint left and be conscious of how it is being used, but a five-year-old may want a gold picture and work away unaware of your concerns.

As with other areas creativity follows a developmental path also. From 0–2 years children enjoy simply experiencing materials, feeling, touching and tasting things. By three to four years they are interested in representing their world but they are not much concerned with the 'realism' of their picture or their model. As the child gets older, to five and six years, realism becomes more important and they enjoy working with smaller equipment and in a more intricate way.

We should try and provide a wide range of creative material and opportunities for young children. We should be non-directive but available as a resource. While it is colourful to have pictures on the wall and mobiles hanging it may not be appropriate to expect the children to make them. Adults who teach children how to draw limit the child's imagination. The use of colouring books, where children are expected to stay 'inside the lines', is restrictive rather than enabling. It does not contribute in any way to a child's artistic development. It may contribute to the development of a child's ability to control a pencil, but if this is the aim of the activity let it be made clear.

Movement, drama and dance: Representation of experiences may not necessarily be through drawing or writing but may be through activity and drama. Young children use movement of body and face as a most articulate form of communication (jumping up and down with joy; stamping in frustration). These expressive movements are the raw material of drama, mime and dance. They capture a mood and give an impression of how a child is reacting to a given situation. Drama is an integral part of the young child's life and drama education for the child must be built along developmental lines. Five-year-olds are at the suitable stage of movement — too structured an activity or too formal a use of apparatus can inhibit their spontaneity.

Children are very confident in their spontaneous dramatic play. In the home corner they can take on roles, switch about with great assurance. They don't play at being the doctor, they are the doctor. As adults we must use this skill within children rather than try to introduce drama forms of our own. We can do this by providing props, dressing-up materials, enrich their experiments, feed in ideas from stories, poetry, art work, extending vocabulary, provide an enabling environment, and allowing the *form* to come from the child. Young children rarely need an audience, the excitement is in the doing. The formal Christmas play or nativity play is on the decrease and this is to be welcomed. It is an adult idea and does not come from young children. It is, of course, enjoyable to tell them the story of the nativity and it is one that will hold their attention. However, representing the story in the form of a playlet is inappropriate to their age. Public celebration is nice but songs, actions and improvisation may be more appropriate than a fixed form of play. By six or seven the actual play will be of interest and have a meaning for the child. Creativity must be facilitated as a means of deepening experiences and not as an attempt to put on a show.

Strengthening a child's sense of 'self': Young children are developing a sense of self and an awareness of others. The relationship between the child and others is important as it is here that a child develops the skills that are so important to future relationship formation. While encouraging social interaction and the expression of feelings a balance between a child's inner world and the outer world must be achieved.

The child's self-concept is affected by experience and is filtered through her perception of how others find her. As adults, we must help children develop a realistic view of self, a view that the child can like and respect. Unless she is liked and respected she cannot like and respect herself. In turn, unless she likes and respects herself it is difficult for her to like and respect others. From a very early age children can pick up their worth and some may come to you with a very damaged or impoverished sense of self. The child's idea of human relationships develops within the context of her own relationships within her world and her relationship with the physical world. Dramatic play and role play is a useful medium for developing the child's awareness of others.

The role of nature: A nature display is helpful in encouraging a sense of the importance of others. It should be used as a resource and not as an ornament. It should be made up of living things that need to be cared for and this helps the child understand the co-operative nature of life and her role within this. Absorption in the pleasure of an event (like falling snow) can lead to self-forgetting. Allowing children the opportunity to wonder at the enchantment of nature, to experience delight and pleasure is very important to their development of a sense of the magical nature of life. In reviewing practice adults should look at how the day meets all the various needs of the child. The importance of the senses, so well expanded in the work of Maria Montessori, must be borne in mind. This can be developed by the use of interest tables with objects that make different noises; with materials that have a different smell or objects that feel different. You can have a taste table or at snack or meal time you can introduce different tastes and different foods for children.

THE ROLE OF THE ADULT

From the above it will be clear that the adult who works with young children has to fulfil a variety of roles. Marion Dowling, in her book *Education 3 to 5: a Teacher's Handbook*, identifies eight such roles: as observer, planner, tutor, conversationalist, questioner, instructor, model and evaluator.

Observer: The skill of observation cannot be overstated and development of this skill has been given a prominent role in this book. One can be trained to observe more effectively and I hope that through practice you have found this to be the case. Observation can be time-consuming but it must be fitted in to the daily routine. Observations should be casual and unobtrusive and go hand in hand with an understanding of child development. Suggestions about developing effective observation have been given in the section on observation in the earlier part of the book.

Planner: Planning is led by observation. Planning the environment is an early requirement and then planning how to spend time, to facilitate social interaction, co-operation and the opportunity for conversation. From your observations you will have information about which children may need your attention more than others and in what way.

Tutor: There are times when an adult can extend children in their play, particularly where children show a difficulty in, say, dramatic play. This bridging role is not intended to direct children but rather tutor them so that they grow in confidence and can initiate their own play in the future.

Conversationalist: Promoting conversation is essential when working with young children. There is research both from Britain and Ireland (see Tizard & Hughes, Hayes) to show that the level of good conversation and dialogue found in services for young children is way below what one would expect. Asking questions to elicit conversation appears to have little valuable effect and leads to dull, single word responses rather than a flow of conversation. The adult who 'chats' to children seems more likely to encourage conversation and often the opportunities arrive at the more mundane level of routine such as tidying up, toilet-time, snack-time and so on.

Questioner: There are a variety of types of question that we use in conversation. There are those that yield a simple 'yes' or 'no' answer such as 'Is this a triangle?' Other questions require more conversation from the children such as 'what do you think might happen next' or 'how do you think Little Bear felt?' Questions can also require the child to think about an issue and then respond: 'Can you remember how many balloons she had?' In asking questions you should avoid asking ones to which you clearly have an answer. Research on questioning suggests that children will answer questions even where they do not understand the question — they seem to understand that a question needs an answer. For this reason you must take care how you formulate questions and what use you make of questioning.

Instructor: During the early years the adult is more of a facilitator than an instructor. We know from studies of cognitive development that children at this stage in development learn more from activity and interaction with their environment and those in it than they do from being given information and told how to do things. For this reason the instructor role is underplayed and the facilitator role emphasised. As children reach the age of seven and eight they are far more receptive to the formal instruction.

Model: We noted earlier that children learn a good deal from observation and imitation. They quickly pick up gestures and tones of voice which we can see in their play. Being aware of our powerful role as model allows us to evaluate our behaviour every now and then. For instance if we expect children to talk quietly we must also talk in a quiet voice. Where children are expected to wear aprons at certain activities, such as cooking, adults should also wear aprons. Modelling appropriate behaviour is one of the more powerful ways of encouraging appropriate behaviour in children. Modelling thinking, for instance, by such comments as 'I needed a new jumper and thought I would like to knit one so I went to the shop and looked at different patterns. When I found a pattern I liked I bought it and then I bought the correct amount of wool'.

Evaluator: Working with young children on a regular basis allows you to keep a record of their progress, evaluate your practice and plan for the future. Regular observation is necessary to gathering the information that will allow you to plan for change. In the next section we will look at some of the information that should be kept and how some can be used to evaluate your practice and children's development.

RECORD KEEPING

The emphasis on discovery/active learning and developmentally appropriate experience for individual children requires adults working with young children to acquire the skill of record-keeping and use of records. It is important to develop an efficient system which does not take up too much time or energy. It should be clear, simple, speedy and efficient. The minimum recorded information that one should keep is well described in a booklet issued by the playgroup movement*. There should be a record card for each child and it should include:

- Full name, address and telephone number of parent/guardian and child.

- Child's date of birth.

- Record of immunisations and allergies and any other significant health information.

- Parents'/guardians' place of employment and telephone number plus carer/childminder where appropriate.

- Name, address and telephone number of family doctor.

- Dietary information

- Any other relevant information, e.g. access or custody arrangements.

The child's own record should be filed in a folder to preserve some examples of her work over time.

As well as the above general records there should also be a system for recording specific incidents. It is recommended, for example, that you keep an Accident Book. This is essential because if details are not recorded immediately they become very blurred. The book should record:

- details of any accident — how many children, how many adults?

- to whom it occurred

- date and time it occurred

- any injury and action taken

- the names of those who witnessed the accident.

This should be entered by the person present at the time of the accident. Parents must always be informed of an accident to their child.

* Taken from *Guidelines of Good Practice for full daycare playgroups.* A PPA publication 1991.

The keeping of records is only useful if you use the material gathered to improve your practice, review your planning or evaluate the progress of the children. Records can be briefly reviewed every weekend with a monthly review involving all the adults concerned. There has been no published research on the use of records in early services in Ireland. A British survey, by Moore and Sylva, of 125 centres found that over half used a recording scheme and used the material to improve their service on all levels. The most common scheme used, apart from the simple record outlined above, was the Keele Preschool Assessment Guide, (KPAG) discussed earlier. This scheme allows you to make a personal record of the behaviour of individual children. You can identify their strengths and weaknesses and, by repeating the assessment every few months, you also get a good progress report. The Keele is not a test, it is a quick scheme for recording behaviour and it simply requires that you record your observations as you feel necessary. Another scheme has been developed by Bates. This is a more standardised system of recording behaviour and practice and, possibly because it is time-consuming, is not so widely used.

Another scale that has been developed is one to measure the quality of daycare services. It is called the Early Childhood Environment Rating Scale (ECERS). This is an American scale but has been used recently in a study in Britain. The scale looks at the quality of the environment, the layout, the materials, routine and activities. It does not look at the behaviour of the children. The researchers who used the scale in Britain found it to be helpful in recording aspects of quality and a valuable guide for assessing practice and planning for the future.

WHO SHOULD SEE YOUR RECORDS?

This is a question that must be asked. Should records be seen by anyone or should they be restricted? If restricted, what criteria do you use? Any service must decide on a policy in this area. The people who might be considered for gaining access could include any staff working with the children; other professionals such as the Public Health Nurse or Social Worker; other agencies or institutions; students and/or parents. There would be general agreement that adults working with the child should have access. Depending on the circumstances it is possible that other professionals should also be allowed access. Students would not automatically have access but they may be allowed limited information as required. Whether parents should have access to records is something that can generate a lot of discussion and debate. Historically parents have tended to be excluded from access to this kind of material.

Over the recent past there has been an increasing emphasis on the importance of collaboration in services and the sharing of information and expertise. At the time of writing there is no requirement on anyone to share records that are written on file. The 1988 Data Protection Act, however, requires that almost all material on computer be on open access. The careful maintaining of records is a useful way of ensuring that you regularly observe children and reassess practice. It acts as a safeguard against complacency and encourages the development of good practice and quality service.

WHAT CONSTITUTES GOOD PRACTICE?

At the beginning of this book I stated that one of my aims was to encourage a move towards a common philosophy of practice so that we could provide the best quality for our children. How can you assess quality? What indicators are there? As there are, at the time of writing, no regulations or standards governing the provision of early services in Ireland it is difficult to estimate what the quality of service is like. It is true that most people working with young children are providing the type of service that they consider best. There has been very little research into quality in Ireland but work coming from the United States and Britain suggests that we can pick out certain factors that are more important than others.

Most people agree that good quality daycare should enhance the development of the child but this involves a value judgment. Are you enhancing the development of a three-year-old by teaching her the letters of the alphabet? Are you restricting the development of a five-year-old if you allow her to experiment and discover without adult direction? Different people will hold different views. In some more adult-led services for the older child adults will say that parents want their child to read before she goes to school. The young child of the 1990s is seen, by developmental psychologists among others, as a competent, complex and active being attempting to understand the world around her. She is a rule tester, even from very early on, and is an active participant in the various relationships she forms. The active nature of the child and her curiosity is seen as an essential ingredient in learning how to learn and think about thinking. Allowing children the opportunity to explore, play, invent, experience and integrate their knowledge through play can be seen as a valuable way of encouraging the development of an independent, coping, adaptable adult. This alters but does not diminish the role of the adult in the lives of the child. Rather than giving information and direction to the child or group of children the adult can now be seen as an important architect of opportunity, providing materials, time and space for the child and supporting the child's learning by being there as a 'scaffolding' to learning. There are other aspects of development that must also be considered, including the issue of relationships, fundamental to the development of the whole child.

How can we assess good quality so that we can strive to provide it? In services dealing with people we must look at dynamic variables as well as the more static ones. Research has identified a variety of important factors of quality. These include the group size, space, ventilation, ratios, training in child development, and the more dynamic factors of behaviour of adults, provision of developmentally appropriate activities and good relationships. These variables are interlinked so that one is more likely to find developmentally appropriate activities where the adults have a basic training and where the ratios are good.

It is not always possible to achieve the ideal but it is always a good idea to aim high. In the important work of caring for and educating young children we must strive to provide the very best we can for them. We must respect children for what they are and not what they will become. While acknowledging what we can do for the child in terms of encouraging and challenging her development and fostering her prosocial skills we must never lose sight of the child in the present, in the here and now. Neither should we lose sight of the whole child, all her aspects and the other people in her life. We must give control to the child in a stable and secure environment so that we can encourage her to move away as a confident child, curious and interested in learning more about the world.

SUMMARY

Applying theory to practice requires careful thought and planning. Consideration of the aims of the services and the needs of the children can guide this task.

Parents are an integral and important part of a child's development. This is recognised by government departments and by voluntary organisations and agencies providing early childhood services. Every effort should be made to encourage parental involvement.

The adult working with young children has a number of distinct roles and their number reflects the complexity of the profession. The roles identified are: observer, planner, tutor, conversationalist, questioner, instructor, model and evaluator. On this last point the keeping of regular records is recommended as a means of evaluating your practice and the service you provide.

At all times adults working in early childhood services must strive to provide a stable, secure and stimulating environment so that the young children in their care have every opportunity to develop to their full potential.

GLOSSARY

Accommodation   A process proposed by Piaget to describe the way a person alters their models/schema to take aboard new knowledge.

Adaptation   A term developed by Piaget to describe the way the organism adapts, adjusts to and alters the environment for survival. This can be both physical and — of more interest to Piaget — mental adaptation.

Anoxia   Lack of oxygen at birth.

Articulation   In terms of language development this refers to a child's level of ability to utter clear and distinctive words.

Assimilation   A process proposed by Piaget to describe the way a person fits in new knowledge with the models or schema already available to that person.

Attachment   The strong bond between a child and significant/familiar figures.

Autonomous   Referring to that stage of moral development where the child appreciates the social nature of rules governing behaviour.

Autosomes   Of the twenty-three pairs of chromosomes, the last, or twenty-third pair, are known as the sex chromosomes. They determine the sex of the individual. The remaining twenty-two pairs of chromosomes are called autosomes.

Baseline level   The normal or usual level of a behaviour or activity.

Behaviour modification   Altering or changing behaviour by the manipulation of environmental factors and the careful use of reinforcement or punishment procedures.

Behaviourist   A school of psychology which studies behaviour in terms of cause (stimulus) and behaviour (response) and which believes that behaviour is learned (and can thus be unlearned).

Biological   All factors affecting the individual from within, factors that are a part of the individual's make-up.

Bonding	A term referring to the very close relationship that forms between mother and infant.
Chromosome	Rod-like structures in the cells which carry the genes. They occur in pairs and there are twenty-three pairs (forty-six chromosomes) in human cells.
CNS	The Central Nervous System — the brain and spinal cord.
Cognition	It refers to the act of knowing, to reason, to be aware — from the Latin *cognito* to apprehend/know. Cognitive Development is the development of the ability to know.
Concept	An idea of a class of objects which can be concrete — 'cups' or (abstract) 'happiness'. Hence conceptualisation — to think in terms of concept.
Concrete operations	This is the third stage of cognitive development as proposed by Piaget and shows a move towards greater conceptualising in thought.
Confidentiality	The maintaining of certain information in confidence.
Conserve	The ability to understand that an object or a liquid does not change its mass or volume simply because it changes shape.
Constructivist	One who believes that we construct reality by our active experience of the environment.
Cross-sectional	A term used to describe research studies that take representatives from a cross-section of a population to study a particular issue.
Curriculum	The content of a course of study — the routine we provide for children can be considered a curriculum.
DNA	Abbreviation for Deoxyribonucleic Acid — the material which makes up the genes.
Decentre	To put oneself in the position of another person, object or time.
Developmentally appropriate	This term refers to activities and experiences that are pitched at a level in line with the abilities of the child.
Dizygotic twins	Referring to twins formed by the separate development of two fertilised eggs — these twins are called fraternal twins.

Dynamic	Active, energetic: in psychology a term to refer to the force to motivate.
Dysfunction	An abnormality of function, where something is not working or functioning as expected.
Early intervention	Term used to describe programmes which aim to effect change by providing services to young children and their families.
Ego	Part of the personality that reacts to reality proposed by Freud.
Egocentric	Centred on self — unable to decentre.
Embryo	The name given to the unborn during the first eight weeks of pregnancy; hence embryonic — of the embryo, early.
Enlightenment	A period, in the eighteenth century, when philosophers placed particular emphasis on reasoning.
Environmental	All factors affecting the individual from without, from the environment.
Enzyme	A protein catalyst which, for example, can act to break down food into different elements during digestion.
Experiment	A test or a trial to establish or demonstrate a fact.
Expressive language	The language which a person can use.
Feral	Wild — this word is used to describe children who have been raised in the wild.
Fertilisation	The process whereby an egg (ovum) is penetrated by a sperm on the first stage towards the development of a new individual.
Fine motor skills	Actions of the smaller muscles — threading, drawing and so on.
Foetus	The name given to the developing, unborn individual after the eighth week of pregnancy.
Formal operations	The fourth and final stage of cognitive development proposed by Piaget. Thinking is now more abstract.

Gamete	The mature germ cell — the ovum or sperm.
Gene	The unit of heredity, carried in the chromosomes. Each gene, or a group of genes, control particular inherited characteristics. Genes can be dominant or recessive.
Genotype	The gene pattern of an individual.
Germ cells	Those cells in the body capable of maturing to become the ova and sperm cells.
Goodness-of-fit	The match between expectations and the reality.
Gross motor skills	Actions of the large muscles — running, jumping and so on.
Headstart	The name given to the programme of preschools developed in the US during the 1960s and 70s, as a means of combating disadvantage through 'compensatory' early education.
Heteronomous	Referring to that stage in moral development where the child believes that rules of behaviour are external to themselves.
Holophrase	A single word which has the meaning of a complete sentence; a one-word sentence.
Id	Inherited instinctive impulses proposed by Freud.
Intuitive thought	A substage of the pre-operational period proposed by Piaget, where children may guess correctly the solution to a problem without a real understanding.
Invariant	Remaining unchanged; for instance, the stages of cognitive development proposed by Piaget always appear in the same order; the order is invariant.
IPPA	Irish Pre-school Playgroups Association.
IQ	Intelligence Quotient — a measure of intellectual performance as measured by standardised tests.
Kindergarten	A type of preschool provision — the name derives from the German *Kinder* (children) and *Garten* (garden). The term originated from Froebel.
LAD	The Language Acquisition Device proposed by Chomsky to explain the innate, inborn characteristics of language.

Libido	Psychic drive or energy associated with the sex instinct, proposed by Freud.
Longitudinal	A term used to describe research studies continuing over a long period of time.
Making strange	Where a child becomes upset at the arrival of a stranger or relative stranger and seeks out a familiar person.
Maladaptive	Not correctly adapted. For example, inappropriate behaviour can be called maladaptive.
Mastery orientation	Towards perfecting a skill or ability.
Maternal	Of or like the mother.
Maturation	The unfolding of inherited potential.
Modelling	To model or provide an example of behaviour.
Monozygotic twins	Referring to twins formed when one fertilised cell divides to form two individuals — the twins are formed from one fertilised cell and are identical.
Moral development	The development of a child's sense of right and wrong, justice and fairness.
Motherese	A particular type of language used between 'good' mothers and their children (it is, of course, not confined to mothers).
Naíonraí	Irish-speaking playgroups.
Naturalistic observation	Observations that occur in the natural environment of the child.
Nature/Nurture	The balance between the influence of heredity and environment on behaviour and development. Also referred to as maturation/learning balance.
NCNA	National Children's Nursery Association.
Nonjudgmental	Withholding judgment about something, someone or some activity observed.
Object permanence	The understanding that objects in the environment have a permanent, independent existence.
Objective	To deal with actual facts in a way that is not influenced by feelings or opinions.

Oedipus Complex	This is where a boy shows attraction to his mother and jealousy of his father. It was proposed by Freud to explain certain characteristics in the behaviour of young children. The female equivalent is called the Electra Complex.
OMEP	The World Organisation for Early Childhood Education. The Irish branch acts as the umbrella group for early childhood care and education in Ireland.
Ovum (Ova)	A biological term used to refer to the female egg which is capable of developing into a new individual following fertilisation.
P.K.U.	Phenylketonuria, a recessive gene-based disorder, which can be controlled by careful diet.
Participatory observation	In which the observer takes an active part in the observation situation. Where the observer remains outside the situation the observation is called non-participatory.
Perception	Action by which the individual reacts to external stimulation. Perceptual development is the development of the ability to perceive.
Phenotype	A set of observable characteristics of the individual determined by genotype and environment.
Placenta	Organ in the uterus which nourishes the foetus attached to it by the umbilical cord.
Playgroup	A preschool service catering for children of three to five years and emphasising the importance of learning through play.
Postmature	Born three or more weeks after the expected date.
Pre-conventional	One of three stages in moral development proposed by Kohlberg — the Pre-conventional, Conventional and Post-Conventional stages.
Pre-linguistic	Before the development of language.
Pre-operational	The second stage of cognitive development proposed by Piaget. Reasoning is influenced by perception.
Preconceptual thought	Thinking that shows poor or inappropriate use of concepts, reflecting an immature conceptual level.

Premature	Born three or more weeks before the expected date.
Prenatal	Referring to the time before birth.
Psychoanalytic	A method for investigating the influence of the unconscious on conscious behaviour.
Psychodynamic	The study of mental and developmental processes from a dynamic point of view.
Psychologist	A person who studies behaviour and the factors influencing behaviour. Different psychologists will approach this task in different ways depending on their particular school of thought.
Psychosexual	Term used to describe the study of the influence of sexuality/libido on psychological development.
Psychosocial	Term used to describe the study of the influence of social factors on psychological development.
Puritanical	With extreme strictness.
Reasoning	Process of solving problems by reference to general principles.
Receptive language	The language which a person understands.
Receptors	Organs which respond to light, heat, sound etc. and transmit signals to sensory nerves.
Reinforcement	Anything that maintains a behaviour is known as reinforcing that behaviour and is called reinforcement.
Reversibility	The ability to think in one direction and back — for example, 2+3=5; 5–3=2. A necessary ability for solving mathematical problems.
Rubella	Also known as 'German measles' this is a virus which can seriously damage the developing foetus, particularly in the first trimester.
Schema	A term Piaget developed to describe the idea of a mental model or plan of the world.
Sensori-motor	The first stage of cognitive development proposed by Piaget; thinking is based in action through sensorial exploration.

Sperm	The male seed which, by fertilising an egg (ovum), contributes to the development of a new individual.
Strange situation	An experimental procedure developed by Mary Ainsworth to assess the strength of attachment in young children.
Super ego	Part of the personality that acts as the conscience of the individual proposed by Freud.
Survey	A research method used to sample the attitudes, opinions, abilities of a group of individuals.
Tabula Rasa	This term literally means a 'blank slate' and was used by Locke to describe the mind of the child at birth. The term was subsequently adopted by the behaviourist school of psychology.
Target Child (TC)	Term used to describe the child at the focus of an observation study.
Telegraphic speech	Early speech which contains the main words of communication, leaving out the less important or redundant words.
Teratogen	The environmental factors that influence or affect the development of the embryo/foetus.
Theoretical	Based on theory — not dealing with facts from experience.
Trimester	The nine months of pregnancy are divided into 3 three-month periods; each period is called a trimester.
Trisomy 21	Better known as Down's Syndrome, this disorder results from the transfer of an extra twenty-first chromosome yielding a complement of forty-seven rather than forty-six chromosomes.
Vicarious learning	To learn by observation rather than direct experience.
Wendy House/Home corner	An area in a playgroup or nursery where children can dress up and play 'house' with the props provided.
Zeitgeist	The spirit of the age — referring to the trend or fashion in a particular period; from the German *Zeit* (time) and *Geist* (spirit).
Zygote	Cell formed by the union of two gametes — an ovum and sperm.

RECOMMENDED READING

Below is a list of various books that I have found useful and informative on the issues considered in this book. The list is not intended to be exhaustive. Although there are topics common to the books, I have grouped them under three headings: Child Development, Early Childhood Care and Education and Play.

CHILD DEVELOPMENT

Athey, C., *Extending Thought in Young Children: A Parent-Teacher Partnership* (London, Paul Chapman Publishing, 1990)

Bee, H., *The Developing Child*, 4th ed., (New York, Harper & Row, 1990)

Berk, L., *Child Development* (Allyn & Bacon, 1989)

Bowlby, J., *Attachment and Loss*: Vol. 1 (London, Hogarth Press, 1969)

Bowlby, J., *Child Care and the Growth of Love* (Harmondsworth, Penguin, 1953)

Bruner, J. and Haste, H. (eds) *Making Sense* (London, Methuen, 1987)

Crystal, D., *Listen to your Child: A Parents' Guide to Children's Language* (Penguin, 1986)

Donaldson, M., *Children's Minds* (Glasgow, Fontana, 1978)

Meadows, S., *Understanding Child Development* (London, Hutchinson, 1986)

Pringle, M. K., *The Needs of Children* (Hutchinson Educational, 1975)

Rutter, M., *Maternal Deprivation Reassessed*, 2nd ed., (Harmondsworth, Penguin, 1981)

Sylva, K. and Lunt, I., *Child Development: A First Course* (Oxford, Blackwell, 1982)

Sylva, K., Roy, C. and Painter, M., *Childwatching at Playgroup and Nursery School* (London, Grant McIntyre, 1980)

Tough, J., *Listening to Children Talking* (London, Ward Lock, 1976)

Wells, G., *Language Development in the Preschool Years* (Cambridge, Cambridge University Press, 1985)

Winnicott, D. W., *The Child, the Family and the Outside World* (Harmondsworth, Penguin, 1964)

EARLY CHILDHOOD CARE AND EDUCATION

Blenkin, G. M. and Kelly, A. V., *Early Childhood Education: A Developmental Curriculum* (London, Paul Chapman Publishing, 1987)

Bruce, T., *Early Childhood Education* (Sevenoaks, Hodder & Stoughton, 1987)

Clark, M., *Children Under Five: Educational Research and Evidence* (London, Gordon & Breach, 1988)

Clarke, M. and Hayes, N., *Child Care in Ireland: A Parent's Guide* (Dublin, Gill & Macmillan, 1991)

Clarke-Stewart, A., *Day Care* (London, Fontana, 1982)

Curtis, A., *A Curriculum for the Preschool Child* (Windsor, NFER & Nelson, 1986)

David, T., *Under Five — Under-educated?* (Buckingham, Open University Press, 1990)

Dowling, M., *Education 3 to 5: A Teacher's Handbook* (London, Paul Chapman Publishing, 1988)

Drummond, M. J., Lally, M. and Pugh, G. (eds), *Working with Children: Developing a Curriculum for the Early Years* (London, NCB, 1989)

Hennessy, E., Martin, S., Moss, P. and Melhuish, E., *Children and Day Care: Lessons From Research* (London, Paul Chapman Publishing, 1992)

Jackson, B. and Jackson, S., *Childminder* (London, Routledge and Kegan Paul, 1979)

Laishley, J., *Working with Young Children* 2nd ed., (London, Hodder & Stoughton, 1987)

McKenna, A., 'Child Care in Ireland 1990' in *Child Care in Ireland: Challenge and Opportunity* (Dublin, EEA, 1990)

McKenna, A., *Childcare and Equal Opportunities: Policies and Services for Childcare in Ireland* (Dublin, EEA, 1988)

Moss, P., *Childcare and Equality of Opportunity* (London, EC, 1988)

Moss, P. and Melhuish, E., (eds) *Current Issues in Day Care for Young Children* (London HMSO, 1991)

Osborn, A. F. and Milbank, J. E., *The Effects of Early Education* (Oxford, Clarendon Press, 1987)

Parry, M. and Archer, H., *Preschool Education* (London, Schools Council/Macmillan Educational, 1974)

Pugh, G. (ed.), *Contemporary Issues in the Early Years* (London, Paul Chapman Publishing/NCB, 1992)

Rouse, D. (ed), *Babies and Toddlers: Carers and Educators. Quality for Under-Threes* (London, NCB, 1991)

Tizard, B. and Hughes, M., *Young Children Learning* (London, Fontana, 1984)

Tobin, T., Wu, D. and Davidson, D., *Preschool in Three Cultures: Japan, China and the United States* (Yale University Press, 1989)

PLAY

Bruce, T., *Time to Play in Early Childhood Education* (Sevenoaks, Hodder & Stoughton, 1991)

Bruner, J., Jolly, A. and Sylva, K. (eds), *Play: its role in development and education* (Harmondsworth, Penguin, 1976)

Garvey, C., *Play*, 2nd ed., (Fontana, 1990)

Hutt, S. J., Tyler, S., Hutt, C. and Christopherson, H., *A Natural History of the Preschool: Exploration, Play and Learning* (London, Routledge, 1989)

Matterson, E. M., *Play with a Purpose for Under-Sevens*, 2nd ed., (Penguin, 1990)

Moyles, J., *Just Playing? The Role and Status of Play in Early Childhood Education* (Milton Keynes, Open University Press, 1989)

Smith, P. K. (ed.), *Children's Play: Research developments and practical application* (New York, Gordon & Breach, 1986)

For suggestions about activities, materials and projects there are many excellent publications available from the Pre-school Playgroups Association in Britain and from the IPPA. Also the Bright Ideas series from Scholastic Publications is full of interesting ideas. Two journals that are valuable are *Child Education* and *Nursery World* — both cover current affairs issues, reviews and project suggestions. The National Children's Bureau in London is also a good source material in the area of early childhood and their address is NCB, Early Childhood Unit, 8 Wakeley Street, London EC1V 7QE.

REFERENCES

INTRODUCTION

E. Lawrence, (ed.), *Friedrich Froebel and English Education* (London, Routledge and Kegan Paul, 1962)

CHAPTER 1

P. Aries, *Centuries of Childhood* (London, Jonathan Cape, 1962)

Department of Health, *Child Care Act* (Dublin, GSO, 1991)

S. Holland, *Rutland Street* (Oxford, Pergamon Press, 1979)

CHAPTER 3

V. Axline, *Dibs: In Search of Self* (Harmondsworth, Penguin, 1971)

A. Bandura, D. Ross, and S. A. Ross, 'Imitation of film-mediated aggressive models' in *Journal of Abnormal Social Psychology*, (Vol. 66, pp. 3–11, 1963)

L. Berk, *Child Development* (Allyn & Bacon, 1989)

M. J. Drummond, and D. Rouse, *Making Assessment Work* (London, NCB, 1992)

J. Laishley, *Working with Young Children*, 2nd ed., (London, Hodder & Stoughton, 1987)

K. Sylva, C. Roy, and M. Painter, *Childwatching at Playgroup and Nursery School* (London, Grant McIntyre, 1980)

S. Tyler, *Keele Preschool Assessment Guide* (Windsor, NFER 1979)

CHAPTER 4

S. Bredekamp, (ed.) *Developmentally Appropriate Practice in Early Childhood Programs Serving Children from Birth through Age Eight*, National Association for the Education of Young Children (NAEYC, 1989)

D. K. Spelt, 'The conditioning of the human fetus in utero' in *Journal of Experimental Psychology*, (Vol. 38, pp. 375–376, 1948)

CHAPTER 5

L. Berk, *Child Development* (Allyn & Bacon, 1989)

T. G. R. Bower, *The Perceptual World of the Child* (London, Fontana, 1977)

A. Curtis, *A Curriculum for the Preschool Child* (Windsor, NFER & Nelson, 1986)

R. Fantz, 'The Origins of Form Perception' in *Scientific American* (Vol. 204, pp. 66–72, 1961)

E. Gibson and R. D. Walk, 'The Visual Cliff' in *Scientific American* (Vol. 202, pp. 64–71, 1960)

CHAPTER 6

M. Donaldson, *Children's Minds* (London, Fontana, 1978)

R. Duska and M. Whelan, *Moral Development: Guide to Piaget and Kohlberg* (Paulist Press, U.S., 1975)

J. Getzels and P. Jackson, *Creativity and Intelligence: Exploration with Gifted Students* (New York, Wiley, 1962)

J. P. Guilford, 'Creativity' in *American Psychologist* (Vol. 4, pp. 444–454, 1950)

L. Kohlberg, 'Moral Stages and Moralisation: the Cognitive-Developmental Approach' in T. Lickona (ed.) *Moral Development and Behaviour: Theory, Research and Social Issues* (New York, Holt, Rinehart and Winston, 1976)

D. Pepler and H. Ross, 'The Effects of Play on Convergent and Divergent Problem solving' in *Child Development* (Vol. 53, pp. 1182–1192, 1981)

J. Piaget, *The Moral Judgment of the Child* (New York, Free Press, 1965 [1932])

M. Wallach, 'Creativity Testing and Giftedness' in F. D. Horowitz & M. O'Brien (eds) *The Gifted and Talented: Developmental Perspectives* (Washington, American Psychological Association, 1985)

CHAPTER 7

N. Chomsky, *Syntactic Structures* (The Hague, Mouton, 1957)

D. Crystal, *Listen to Your Child: A Parents' Guide to Children's Language* (Harmondsworth, Penguin, 1986)

C. E. Snow, 'The development of conversation between mothers and babies' in K. Sylva and I. Lunt's *Child Development: A First Course* (London, Grant McIntyre, 1980)

CHAPTER 8

B. E. Andersson, 'Effects of public daycare — a longitudinal study' in *Child Development* (Vol. 60, pp. 857–866, 1989)

J. Bowlby, *Childcare and the Growth of Love* (Harmondsworth, Penguin 1953)

E. Erikson, *Childhood and Society* (New York, Norton, 1950)

A. Freud and S. Dann, An Experiment in group upbringing from 'The Psychoanalytic Study of the Child' in K. Sylva and I. Lundt's *Child Development: A First Course* (London, Grant McIntyre, 1980)

K. Grossman, *et al*, 'Maternal sensitivity and newborns' — orientation responses as related to quality of attachment in Northern Germany (1985) in L. Berk's *Child Development* (Allyn & Bacon, 1989)

M. Rutter, *Maternal Deprivation Reassessed*, 2nd ed., (Harmondsworth, Penguin, 1981)

A. Thomas and S. Chess, *Temperament and Development* (New York, Brunner/Mazel, 1977)

CHAPTER 9

Department of Health, *Child Abuse Checklist* available from The Childcare Section, Hawkins House, Dublin 2.

CHAPTER 10

T. Bruce, *Time to Play in Early Childhood Education* (London, Hodder and Stoughton, 1991)

A. Curtis, *A Curriculum for the Preschool Child* (Windsor, NFER & Nelson, 1986)

S. J. Hutt, S. Tyler, C. Hutt and H. Christopherson, *A Natural History of the Preschool: Exploration, Play and Learning* (London, Routledge, 1989)

A. F. Osborn and J. E. Milbank, *The Effects of Early Education* (Oxford, Clarendon Press, 1987)

M. Parry and H. Archer, *Preschool Education* (London, Schools Council/Macmillan Educational, 1974)

K. Sylva, 'Educational Aspects of Daycare in England and Wales', in *Current Issues in Daycare for Young Children* (Peter Moss and Edward Melhuish, eds) (London, HMSO, 1991)

L. Vygotsky, *Mind and Society* (Cambridge M A, Harvard University Press, 1978)

CHAPTER 11

A. Curtis, *A Curriculum for the Preschool Child* (Windsor, NFER & Nelson, 1986)

T. David, *Under Five — Under-educated?* (Buckingham, Open University Press, 1990)

Department of Education, *Education for a Changing World: Green Paper* (Dublin, GSO, 1992)

M. Donaldson, *Children's Minds* (London, Fontana, 1978)

M. Dowling, *Education 3 to 5: a Teacher's Handbook* (London, Paul Chapman Publishing, 1988)

N. Hayes, 'State-aided Day Nurseries: an Exploratory Study' (unpublished M. Ed. thesis, University of Dublin, Trinity College, 1983)

S. Jowett and K. Sylva 'Does kind of preschool matter?' in *Educational Research* (Vol. 28, pp. 21–31, 1986)

M. Parry and H. Archer, *Preschool Education* (London, Schools Council/ Macmillan Educational, 1974)

Pre-school Playgroups Association (PPA) *Guidelines of Good Practice for Full Daycare Playgroups* (PPA, 1991)

M. K. Pringle, *The Needs of Children* (London, Hutchinson Educational, 1975)

B. Tizard and M. Hughes, *Young Children Learning* (London, Fontana, 1984)

S. Tyler, *Keele Preschool Assessment Guide* (Windsor, NFER, 1979)

INDEX